AF706500

Cyber Shield

Mastering Social Media Safety in a Digital World

Nathan Venture, D.

Copyright 2026 All rights reserved.

No part of this book may be reproduced in any form or by any electronic or mechanical means including information storage and retrieval systems, without permission in writing from the author. The only exception is by a reviewer, who may quote short excerpts in a review.

Although the author and publisher have made every effort to ensure that the information in this book was correct at press time, the author and publisher do not assume and hereby disclaim any liability to any party for any loss, damage, or disruption caused by errors or omissions, whether such errors or omissions result from negligence, accident, or any other cause.

This publication is designed to provide accurate and authoritative information with regard to the subject matter covered. It is sold with the understanding that the publisher is not engaged in rendering professional services. If legal advice or other expert assistance is required, the services of a competent professional should be sought.

The fact that an organization or website is referred to in this work as a citation and/or a potential source of further information does not mean that the author or the publisher endorses the information the organization or website may provide or recommendations it may make.

Please remember that Internet websites listed in this work may have changed or disappeared between when this work was written and when it is read.

Contents

Introduction

Before you change any setting or memorize any checklist, pause long enough to understand the shape of the problem. Social media security is not only about keeping strangers out of an account. It is about controlling what your profile reveals, what your behavior suggests, and what your connected tools quietly expose. A platform account can be protected with a strong password and still leave you vulnerable if your public posts reveal routines, your recovery email is weak, or a third-party app has broad access to your data.

The risk is also more fluid than it used to be. Social platforms now blend messaging, publishing, commerce, advertising, customer service, and identity verification into one environment. That convergence creates convenience, but it also creates more ways for attackers to enter. A single compromised login can expose conversations, payment details, brand assets, contact lists, and trust relationships all at once. For individuals, that may mean embarrassment, stalking, fraud, or identity misuse. For businesses and creators, it can mean lost revenue, damaged credibility, and time spent proving that a message, post, or request was not actually yours.

One reason this environment is so effective for attackers is that social media is built around visibility and interaction. People are encouraged to respond quickly, share openly, and connect broadly. Those habits are useful for growth, but they also reward impulsive behavior. A rushed click, a public birthday, a location tag, or a reused password can become the opening an attacker needs. Security in this context is not about withdrawing from the platform. It is about being deliberate enough to decide what should be public, what should be limited, and what should never be exposed in the first place.

It helps to think of social media safety as a layered discipline. The first layer is account access: passwords, authentication, recovery methods, and session control. The second layer is privacy: who can see posts, contact you, tag you, or discover your profile. The third layer is content and behavior: what your posts reveal, how you verify requests, and how consistently you manage your online identity. The fourth layer is the ecosystem around the account: phones, laptops, browser extensions, scheduling tools, analytics platforms, and any service that can read or publish on your behalf. Weakness in any one of these layers can undermine the rest.

That is why the most effective approach starts with awareness rather than tools. You need to know which accounts matter most, what kinds of information would cause the most harm if exposed, and where your habits may be creating unnecessary risk. Some readers will find that their biggest exposure comes from oversharing. Others will discover that the real problem is a forgotten login on an old device, a recycled password, or an app they granted access to years ago and never reviewed again. The details differ, but the principle is the same: you cannot secure what you have not identified.

As you move through the rest of this book, keep one idea in mind: social media safety is a working process, not a one-time fix. Platforms change, attackers adapt, and your own online footprint grows over time. The goal is to build habits that keep pace with that change without turning every post or login into a burden. When security becomes part of how you use social media, rather than an afterthought, you reduce risk without giving up the benefits of being visible online.

CHAPTER 1

Chapter 1: The New Risk Landscape of Social Media

Social media no longer sits at the edge of daily life; it has become a central layer of communication, promotion, customer service, and personal expression, which means the risks attached to it now reach far beyond the app itself. A single profile can reveal enough context to help an attacker choose a target, imitate a voice, or move from one connected service to another. At the same time, the speed and informality that make these platforms useful also make them easy to misuse, especially when trust is built quickly and checked slowly.

How social media changed the attack surface for individuals and organizations

Social media changed the attack surface by turning ordinary behavior into usable intelligence. In the past, an attacker often needed a technical foothold first: a stolen password, a compromised server, or physical access to a device. Now, a person or organization can be profiled from public posts, follower lists, comments, tagged photos, bios, event check-ins, and even the timing of activity. What used to be scattered clues are now assembled into a detailed picture of identity, routine, relationships, and trust. That picture helps an attacker decide whom to target, what story to tell, and which pressure point is most likely to work.

For individuals, the danger is not just that a profile is visible. It is that a profile is readable. A birthday post can help answer a recovery question. A vacation update can reveal when a home is empty. A photo of a badge, a school name, a license plate, or a workspace can expose location and affiliation. A casual comment thread can reveal who you trust, who you work with, and what topics make you respond quickly. Social platforms compress all of this into a format that is easy for humans to scan and easy for attackers to mine. The result is a lower barrier to reconnaissance, which is the phase where adversaries gather information before they strike.

Organizations face a broader version of the same problem. A company's social presence is no longer just a marketing channel; it is a public operations layer. Customer service replies, recruitment posts, executive announcements, product launches, and behind-the-scenes content all create openings for social engineering. Attackers can imitate brand tone, study response habits, and identify staff members who handle money, support, or access requests. They can also use the organization's own content to make fraudulent messages feel legitimate. If a business regularly posts about shipping delays, account changes, or seasonal promotions, those themes can be repurposed into convincing scams. The public-facing nature of social media means that the same channels used to build trust can also be used to exploit it.

The attack surface also expanded because social media encourages connection by default. Friend requests, follows, group invites, DMs, mentions, and collaborative features are designed to reduce friction. That design is useful for engagement, but it also gives attackers more paths in. A malicious account does not need to break down a single fortified door if it can blend into a network, impersonate a peer, or exploit a moment of attention. Once inside the conversation stream, an attacker can move from public content to private messages, from messages to links, and from links to credential theft or malware delivery. In this environment, trust is not a fixed asset; it is something that can be simulated, borrowed, or redirected.

This shift is especially important because social media activity rarely stays contained within the platform. Posts are cross-shared, screenshots circulate, usernames are reused, and profile details are copied into other services. A single account can become a bridge between personal, professional, and financial systems. That is why a social profile should be viewed as part of a larger digital ecosystem rather than as an isolated page. Research on cyber harm emphasizes that attacks often propagate across interconnected systems, creating effects that extend well beyond the first point of compromise [17]. On social media, that propagation can begin with a simple interaction and end with reputational damage, credential theft, or access to connected tools.

Newer technologies have made the attack surface even more flexible. Deepfakes and other forms of synthetic media can be used to imitate a person's voice or appearance, making it harder to trust what is seen or heard online [4]. At the same time, advances in artificial intelligence can help attackers automate personalization, scale impersonation, and adapt messages to specific audiences [5]. For users and organizations, this means the old assumption that "I would recognize a fake" is no longer reliable. A convincing message may be built from real photos, real names, real writing patterns, and real context, all stitched together into a false request. The threat is not only technical deception; it is social and psychological manipulation at scale.

The practical consequence is that social media security must account for exposure, not just access. A locked account can still reveal enough to support fraud, impersonation, harassment, or targeted intrusion. Privacy settings help, but they do not erase the information already shared, copied, or inferred. Every public profile, tagged image, and active comment thread adds to the map an attacker can build. That map is what makes social media different from older communication tools: it does not merely host messages, it continuously generates intelligence. Protecting yourself or your organization therefore begins with understanding that the attack surface is made not only of software and passwords, but also of visibility, relationships, habits, and the stories your online presence tells.

Common threat types: phishing, impersonation, account takeover, and data harvesting

Phishing remains one of the most reliable ways to get a person to hand over access voluntarily. On social media, it rarely looks like a generic scam email. It is more often a direct message that appears to come from a platform, a brand partner, a customer, a follower, or even a friend whose account has already been compromised. The message may warn that your account will be suspended, that a payment is pending, that a post violates policy, or that you need to "verify" something immediately. The goal is not usually to trick you with technical sophistication; it is to interrupt your judgment long enough to make you click, log in, or share a code. Because social platforms encourage fast replies and casual interaction, phishing messages can blend into normal activity more easily than they do in email.

Impersonation is the next layer of abuse, and it is especially dangerous because it exploits trust that has already been built. Attackers may copy a profile photo, reuse a display name, imitate writing style, or create a nearly identical account with one altered character in the handle. In some cases, the goal is broad fraud: asking followers for gift cards, cryptocurrency, or urgent help. In others, the impersonation is more deliberate and scalable, with attackers using harvested profile details, device and behavioral fingerprints, and other metadata to make fake identities more convincing [24]. That means the threat is not limited to celebrity-level accounts. Small businesses, creators, and local service providers are often easier to clone because their audiences are smaller, their verification habits may be looser, and their customers may be less suspicious of a familiar-looking message.

Account takeover is what happens when the attacker moves from pretending to be you to becoming you. Once inside, the intruder can reset recovery details, change contact information, send messages from a trusted account, and use that credibility to spread the compromise further. A takeover may begin with a stolen password, but it can also follow a phishing login page, a reused password from another breach, or a malicious app that captures session data. Mobile devices are part of this picture as well, because attackers increasingly target the way people authenticate, approve prompts, and manage accounts from phones and tablets [23]. The risk is not only the loss of access. A compromised social account can be used to damage reputation, solicit money, spread malware, or lock legitimate owners out long enough to cause real business harm.

Data harvesting is quieter, but it often fuels everything else. Here the attacker may not need to break in at all. Public profiles, bios, photo captions, comments, tagged images, follower lists, and location clues can be collected at scale to build a detailed picture of a person's identity, habits, relationships, and likely security questions. That information can support targeted phishing, impersonation, and password-reset abuse. It can also help attackers identify who has access to what, which is why digital identity management has become more difficult in cloud-connected, highly distributed environments [26]. In practice, harvesting turns ordinary social activity into a long-term intelligence source. A birthday post can help with account recovery guessing. A vacation photo can reveal when a person is away. A staff directory post can identify the employee most likely to approve a request.

These threat types often work together rather than separately. A harvested profile makes a phishing message more believable. A successful phishing attempt makes impersonation easier. A takeover gives the attacker a trusted account to harvest more data from the victim's network. This chain reaction is one reason identity misuse continues to impose serious financial and non-financial costs on victims and organizations [25]. It is also why social media security cannot focus only on passwords or only on privacy settings. The attacker is looking for the easiest route through the whole system: human trust, public information, weak recovery options, and overexposed connections.

One useful way to think about these threats is by the kind of trust they exploit. Phishing abuses urgency and authority. Impersonation abuses familiarity and social proof. Account takeover abuses stored trust, such as saved sessions, recovery channels, and automatic recognition by followers. Data harvesting abuses openness itself, turning harmless-looking content into a dossier. The response, then, is not just to "be careful" in a vague sense. It is to slow down any request that pressures you to act quickly, verify identities through a second channel when something matters, limit what strangers can infer from your profile, and treat every connected account as part of the same security surface.

For individuals, the practical implication is that every public detail should be evaluated for what it reveals to someone who does not already know you. For businesses and creators, the implication is broader: the brand voice, customer expectations, and staff workflows all become part of the attack surface. A fake support account can exploit customer frustration. A cloned creator profile can steal audience attention. A compromised employee account can lend credibility to a malicious request. The more visible and responsive your presence is, the more important it becomes to make verification routine instead of exceptional.

Why small businesses, creators, and everyday users are all attractive targets

Small businesses, creators, and everyday users are attractive targets for the same reason: they all hold something valuable, but they usually hold it in ways that are easier to reach than a heavily guarded enterprise system. Attackers do not need every target to be rich in the traditional sense. They need targets that are accessible, responsive, and likely to make fast decisions under pressure. A small business account may connect directly to customers, payment tools, and a public reputation. A creator account may connect to sponsorships, audience trust, and a recognizable voice. An everyday user may connect to family, private conversations, location patterns, and other accounts that can be leveraged for fraud. In each case, the account is not just a profile; it is a doorway.

For small businesses, the value often lies in operational access and customer trust. A social account can be used to answer inquiries, announce promotions, handle complaints, and drive traffic to a store or website. That makes the account a practical business asset, but also a high-leverage target. If an attacker takes over a business page, they can send fake invoices, post fraudulent links, change contact details, or impersonate support staff. Even without full takeover, they can exploit the fact that customers expect a quick response. A convincing message that appears to come from the brand can redirect payments, harvest credentials, or create confusion that costs time and money. Smaller organizations are especially vulnerable because one person often manages posting, messages, ads, and recovery settings at once, so there are fewer layers of review before a mistake becomes public.

Creators face a different but equally serious risk profile. Their accounts are built on visibility, consistency, and direct engagement, which means their public presence is part of the product. That visibility brings opportunity, but it also gives attackers a rich set of signals to imitate tone, timing, and relationships. A creator's audience may be trained to respond quickly to limited-time offers, exclusive content, or urgent updates, which makes impersonation especially effective. Attackers can also exploit the business side of creator work: sponsorship inquiries, affiliate links, media requests, and brand negotiations. A fake partner message or a compromised collaborator account can open the door to credential theft or payment diversion. When a creator's reputation is tied to authenticity, even a short-lived breach can damage audience confidence in ways that are difficult to repair.

Everyday users are often underestimated because they do not see themselves as high-value targets. That assumption is exactly what makes them useful to attackers. A personal account may reveal enough to support identity theft, account recovery abuse, social engineering, or targeted fraud against friends and relatives. It may also be used as a stepping-stone into other services. If someone reuses passwords, ignores login alerts, or leaves recovery options weak, a social media compromise can spread into email, shopping, cloud storage, or financial accounts. In addition, ordinary users frequently have networks of trust that attackers can exploit. A message that appears to come from a friend, sibling, coworker, or classmate often gets more attention than a generic scam attempt. That trust can be used to spread malicious links, request money, or collect personal details with very little resistance.

There is also a scale advantage for attackers. A single compromised account may not be worth much by itself, but thousands of ordinary accounts can be automated, monetized, or used in coordinated campaigns. Criminal groups often rely on repetition rather than sophistication. They send the same lure to many people, then focus on the few who respond. This is why “low-profile” users still matter. The attacker does not need to know who has the most money; they need to know who is likely to click, reply, or comply. Research on cybercriminal transactional methods shows that online crime is organized around practical opportunities for conversion and payment, not just around technical complexity [38]. Social platforms make that conversion easier because communication, identity, and trust are already bundled together.

A final reason these groups are targeted is that they each face pressure to act quickly. Small businesses want to keep customers happy. Creators want to stay visible and responsive. Everyday users want to help, confirm, or protect people they care about. Attackers know this and design messages to trigger urgency, embarrassment, curiosity, or fear. A fake copyright complaint, a false verification notice, a “business partner” needing an immediate update, or a “friend” asking for help can all push someone to bypass normal caution. Artificial intelligence can make these messages more convincing and scalable, lowering the effort needed to produce persuasive social engineering at volume [33]. The result is not that one group is inherently careless; it is that each group has a normal workflow an attacker can imitate.

The common thread is that social media accounts are rarely isolated. They sit at the intersection of identity, communication, and access. For businesses, that intersection includes customers and revenue. For creators, it includes audience trust and brand value. For everyday users, it includes private relationships and personal data. That is why attackers keep coming back to these targets: the payoff is not limited to the account itself. It extends into the people, tools, and decisions connected to it.

The hidden cost of oversharing, weak settings, and public-by-default behavior

The danger in oversharing is not limited to one embarrassing post or one overly open profile. It is cumulative. A harmless-looking bio, a vacation photo, a routine check-in, a workplace mention, and a birthday post about a family member can combine into a pattern that tells a stranger far more than any single item would. Modern privacy problems are often built from these fragments. Research on digital identity exposure shows that people routinely leave identifiable traces across platforms without fully recognizing the long-term implications [43]. That matters because attackers do not need a perfect dossier; they need enough detail to make a message believable, a guess accurate, or a target worth the effort.

Oversharing also creates a kind of social proof for attackers. The more a profile reveals about your relationships, habits, opinions, and interests, the easier it becomes to imitate your voice or predict what you will respond to. If someone knows where you work, who you work with, what you sell, when you travel, or which causes you care about, they can tailor a request that feels personal and urgent. That is why public information is not harmless just because it was willingly posted. Once it is assembled, it becomes a tool for manipulation. A scammer can reference a recent trip, a new product launch, a family event, or a complaint you made in comments and use that detail to lower your guard.

Weak settings make that problem worse by turning accidental exposure into default exposure. Many platforms are designed to maximize sharing, discovery, and engagement, not restraint. If privacy controls are left untouched, the platform may assume you want broad visibility, easy searchability, location tagging, open comments, and quick reuse of your content. In practice, that means the burden is on you to reduce access rather than grant it. A profile that is "public by default" can expose far more than the owner intended, especially when old settings remain in place after platform updates or when new features are enabled without review. Security failures often begin not with a dramatic breach, but with an overlooked option that quietly broadens the audience.

For individuals, the hidden cost shows up in reputation, safety, and unwanted attention. A post that reveals your neighborhood, child's school, daily commute, or upcoming absence from home can create real-world risk. Even less sensitive details can have a cost when they are used to profile your behavior. Frequent posting times can suggest when you are online. Repeated location tags can reveal travel habits. Public comments can expose relationships, preferences, and emotional triggers. Over time, this information can be used for stalking, harassment, impersonation, or targeted fraud. The harm is not always immediate, which is part of what makes it easy to ignore. A single exposure may seem minor; the pattern becomes dangerous later.

For small businesses and creators, the cost often appears as lost trust and operational exposure. A public-facing account is not just a social presence; it can be a gateway to customers, payment tools, brand reputation, and internal workflows. If posts reveal staff names, vendor relationships, schedules, or the structure of a team, an attacker can use that information to impersonate support, pressure employees, or target the right person with a convincing request. Public comments and direct messages can also be mined for service issues, complaints, and emotional pressure points. In that sense, oversharing does not merely reveal content. It reveals process. And process is often what an attacker needs to bypass careful people.

Weak settings also create a false sense of control. People often assume that because they did not accept a stranger as a friend, or because they rarely post personal details, their account is sufficiently protected.

But privacy on social media is rarely binary. A profile can be partially visible, searchable, taggable, recommendable, and still expose enough to be useful to an attacker. Public-by-default behavior is especially risky because it normalizes exposure one setting at a time. If your account allows anyone to message you, tag you, reshare your content, or discover you through contact syncing, then your presence is being distributed beyond the audience you may have in mind. The result is not just more visibility. It is more pathways for abuse.

There is also a psychological cost that people often overlook. When a profile is highly exposed, users may begin to self-censor in response to the possibility of being watched, copied, judged, or targeted. That can affect how a person communicates, what a business publishes, and how quickly someone reacts to suspicious contact. In privacy law, scholars have long recognized that invasions of privacy can produce both reputational and psychic harm [41]. On social media, that harm is intensified because the audience is large, the content is persistent, and the boundary between personal and public is easy to blur. The more you leave open by habit, the more energy you spend managing the consequences.

The practical lesson is not to disappear from social media. It is to treat visibility as a resource that should be assigned deliberately. Before posting, it helps to ask what the content reveals about location, routine, relationships, finances, work structure, or future plans. Before leaving settings untouched, it helps to ask whether the platform is optimizing for your safety or for its own reach. And before assuming a post is harmless, it helps to remember that attackers are not looking at one item in isolation. They are looking for patterns, openings, and signals they can reuse. The hidden cost of oversharing is that it hands them those pieces for free.

CHAPTER 2

Chapter 2: Understanding What You're Really Protecting

Before you can secure an account, you have to recognize what that account represents. A social profile is not just a login; it is a bundle of identity signals, public credibility, and relationships that can be borrowed, distorted, or used against you. For an individual, that may mean the difference between being seen as authentic or suspicious, reachable or unreachable, trusted or ignored. For a creator or business, it can also affect customer confidence, partner relationships, and the ability to speak with authority at all. The real task here is to separate what is merely visible from what is truly sensitive, because attackers rarely need everything to cause damage.

Digital identity, reputation, and trust as core security assets

Security work becomes much more effective when you stop thinking only about passwords and start thinking about assets. On social media, the most fragile assets are often not files or devices but the things that make other people willing to believe, follow, hire, buy, or respond: your identity, your reputation, and the trust attached to both. If an attacker cannot read your messages, they may still succeed by making others doubt you, impersonate you, or treat your account as unreliable. That is why a compromised profile can create harm long before anyone notices a login alert. Cyber harm is not limited to technical loss; it spreads into social, financial, and operational damage [17].

Digital identity is the version of you that platforms, followers, customers, and search engines can observe and rank. It includes your name, handle, profile image, bio, posting style, contact methods, and the network of accounts linked to you. It also includes the patterns that make your account recognizable: when you post, how you reply, which topics you discuss, and what kinds of requests you accept. That identity can be copied with surprising accuracy. A fake account does not need to be perfect; it only needs to be convincing long enough to extract attention, money, access, or private information. For businesses and creators, the identity layer is especially important because it is often the first filter people use before deciding whether to engage.

Reputation is the judgment others make about whether your account is safe, competent, and authentic. It is built slowly and damaged quickly. A single fraudulent post, an embarrassing reply, a hacked story, or a public argument can reduce confidence in ways that are hard to reverse. Reputation damage matters because social platforms run on attention and credibility. When trust drops, engagement falls, support requests increase, and legitimate messages are ignored. In practice, this means a security incident is never just an IT problem. It can affect sales, partnerships, client relationships, and the willingness of your audience to act on future posts.

Trust is the operational value that makes your account useful in the first place. People trust your name, your voice, your verification status, your history, and the expectation that you will not abuse the channel. Attackers understand this and routinely try to borrow it. They may send a payment request from a copied profile, announce a fake giveaway, or use a compromised account to ask followers for urgent help. The message works because it arrives wrapped in a familiar identity. This is why impersonation is so effective: it does not need to defeat technology if it can defeat confidence.

Once you view identity, reputation, and trust as security assets, certain behaviors become easier to evaluate. A post is not only content; it is a signal. A comment is not only engagement; it is a public association. A connected app is not only convenient; it is a delegated trust relationship. The same logic applies to brand voice. If your account suddenly sounds unlike itself, followers may hesitate even if the post is harmless. If your business account is used inconsistently by multiple people, the absence of a clear voice can itself become a vulnerability, because it gives attackers room to blend in or create confusion.

These assets also interact with each other. Weak identity controls make reputation easier to damage. Damaged reputation makes trust harder to recover. Lost trust increases the impact of every future message, because people become less certain about what is real. That is why a good social media security plan does more than prevent account takeover. It protects the signals that make your account believable. It limits the chances that your name, image, and history can be used out of context or turned against you. It also reduces the amount of recovery work you must do if something goes wrong, because a clear and consistent identity is easier to defend than a scattered one.

For individuals, this may mean treating your public profile as a professional surface even when you use it casually. For creators, it may mean protecting the specific cues that followers rely on to recognize authentic communication. For small businesses, it may mean making sure customer-facing accounts have clear ownership, consistent naming, and a documented approval path for posts and replies. In all cases, the key question is the same: if someone tried to imitate you today, what would they copy first, and what would your audience use to tell the difference? The answer to that question reveals where your real security work begins.

Personal data, location clues, and behavioral patterns attackers can exploit

Attackers rarely need a full dossier to make progress. They usually need enough fragments to answer three questions: who you are, where you tend to be, and how you behave when you are online. Public profiles, tagged photos, story replies, bios, recurring hashtags, and even the tone of your comments can supply those fragments. What looks like casual self-expression to you can become a reliable intelligence source to someone mapping your life. Online social deception thrives on this kind of piecing together, because the more believable the context, the easier it is to manipulate the target [68].

Personal data is not limited to obvious items like your full name, email address, or phone number. A determined attacker also values the smaller details that help verify identity or predict responses. A birthday post can narrow down security questions. A workplace mention can reveal your employer, role, or likely internal contacts. A school name can expose alumni networks or old passwords based on familiar themes. Even a profile photo may provide clues about uniforms, badges, home decor, vehicle models, or family members. When enough of these details are combined, they support impersonation, account recovery abuse, or tailored phishing attempts that feel specific enough to be trusted.

Location clues are especially useful because they turn a static profile into a live map. A check-in, a geotagged image, a caption about commuting, or a repeated mention of a favorite gym, café, or neighborhood can reveal where you spend time and when you are likely absent. Attackers do not need your exact address to benefit from this. They may use location patterns to time a scam message, guess when a business is closed, identify when a creator is traveling, or determine whether a home is empty. For small businesses, location clues can also expose store hours, delivery routines, and staffing patterns that make social engineering easier. In some cases, the goal is not immediate theft but long-term observation, which is why routine location sharing deserves the same caution as direct contact information.

Behavioral patterns are often the most overlooked source of risk because they feel harmless in isolation. The times you post, the speed at which you reply, the accounts you engage with, and the subjects that reliably get your attention all create a usable pattern. If you always answer DMs within minutes, an attacker can exploit urgency. If you regularly post after hours, they can time a fake support message when you are tired and less careful. If you tend to repost content from specific partners or vendors, a spoofed message from one of those accounts may seem routine. Behavioral profiling is powerful because it helps an attacker choose the right pressure point: urgency for one person, flattery for another, authority for a third.

These patterns also help attackers sound familiar. A message that references your recent trip, your last livestream, your child's school event, or your latest product launch feels personalized because it is personalized. That is the point. Social engineering becomes more effective when it uses details drawn from your own public trail. Research on online deception shows that social platforms give attackers a rich environment for building trust, imitation, and manipulation at scale [68]. The same public traces that help you connect with an audience can help someone else build a convincing pretext.

For creators and businesses, the risk extends beyond the account holder. Personal data, location clues, and behavioral patterns can reveal team structure, response habits, and operational weak points. A public comment thread may show who handles customer complaints. A repeated posting schedule may show when no one is watching the account closely. A shared location tag may reveal the office, studio, or event space where staff can be approached or impersonated. If your brand voice is highly consistent, that consistency can be useful for marketing but also for attackers trying to imitate your tone in a fake support message or fraudulent partnership request. AI-assisted impersonation and deepfake techniques are making this kind of deception more scalable and more convincing [61][62].

The practical lesson is not to disappear from social media. It is to stop treating every detail as isolated. One post may be harmless; ten posts may reveal a pattern. One location tag may be convenient; repeated tags may show a routine. One friendly reply may be ordinary; a consistent response style may become a signature that others can copy. When you review your own presence, ask what a stranger could infer by collecting your public fragments over time. The more easily those fragments answer questions about identity, place, and behavior, the more carefully they should be shared.

Business value tied to followers, customers, brand voice, and access

For a small business, a creator account, or even a personal profile that has become a public-facing identity, followers are not just a vanity metric. They are an audience, a distribution channel, and often the first layer of trust between you and the people who buy from you, recommend you, or rely on you. If an attacker gains control of that account, the immediate damage is not limited to lost access. They can speak to your audience in your name, redirect traffic, spread false offers, damage relationships, and undermine the confidence that took time to build. In that sense, followers are part of the asset base, because they determine how quickly your message travels and how believable it appears when it arrives.

Customers are even more directly tied to business value. A social account may be the place where people ask questions before purchasing, confirm whether a promotion is real, or decide whether a brand is responsive and trustworthy. That makes the account a front door, not a side channel. If a scammer uses the profile to post a fake sale, send fraudulent payment instructions, or collect customer information through a convincing message, the harm can extend beyond the platform into refunds, chargebacks, support costs, and legal exposure. The account may also contain customer conversations, order details, or service complaints that reveal patterns an attacker can exploit for social engineering. A business that treats its social presence as merely promotional often misses that it is also operational infrastructure.

Brand voice is another security asset because it shapes recognition. People learn the rhythm of a business: the words it uses, the tone it avoids, the kinds of questions it answers, and the way it responds under pressure. Attackers know this. They do not need to copy a logo perfectly if they can imitate the style well enough to sound plausible. That is why sudden changes in language, promotional style, or response patterns can be a warning sign to followers and to internal staff. Deepfake and synthetic media research has shown how convincingly digital content can imitate real people and real communication styles, which raises the stakes for any account that depends on public trust [71]. When your voice is consistent, deviations stand out more clearly. When your voice is sloppy or undefined, impersonation becomes much easier.

Access is the most obvious business value, but it is also the most underestimated. A social account may connect to scheduling tools, storefronts, ad managers, analytics dashboards, email systems, or team inboxes. One compromised login can become a pathway into many other services. For a small business, that can mean an attacker not only posts on your behalf but also changes passwords, removes collaborators, or locks the real owner out during a critical sales window. The practical risk is compounded when multiple people share access without clear role boundaries. In those environments, the account is no longer just a marketing asset; it is a control point for communication, sales, and sometimes payment. That is why access management deserves the same attention as content strategy.

This is also where the business and reputational sides of social media overlap. A compromised account can be used to manipulate public perception, not just to steal data. False announcements, fabricated endorsements, and misleading claims can travel quickly because they appear to come from a legitimate source. Research on misinformation and manipulation in digital media shows that false content spreads effectively when it exploits attention, emotion, and cognitive shortcuts [72]. For a business, that means an attacker does not need to convince everyone forever; they only need enough people to believe the false post long enough to act on it. A rumor about a product recall, a fake giveaway, or an urgent refund request can create confusion before anyone has time to verify it.

Creators and brands that rely on high engagement face an additional layer of exposure: the audience often expects immediacy. That expectation can be turned against them. A rushed response, a hurried click, or a public correction made too late can amplify the harm. Virtual and synthetic personas make this problem even more complex, because the line between real, curated, and manufactured identity is already blurred in many feeds [73]. If your account is part of a business model, the security question is not only whether the login is protected. It is whether the account can continue to represent the business accurately when pressure, deception, or compromise enters the picture.

It helps to think in terms of what would be costly to lose, distort, or misuse. For some accounts, the most sensitive asset is the follower base itself, because rebuilding reach takes time. For others, it is customer trust, because one fraudulent post can damage months of careful work. For others still, it is brand voice, because consistency is what makes the account recognizable. And for many, it is access, because the account sits at the intersection of communication and operations. Once you identify which of those values matters most, your security decisions become more precise. You can decide which accounts need the strongest authentication, which team members need limited permissions, which messages require approval, and which connected tools should be removed entirely if they do not clearly support the business.

Mapping your most sensitive accounts, content, and connected services

The first step is to stop thinking of your social presence as one account and start seeing it as a network of exposure points. Some of those points are obvious: the profile that carries your name, your main email address, your direct messages, and the content you publish publicly. Others are less visible but often more sensitive: recovery emails, phone numbers, linked business tools, ad accounts, cloud storage, payment services, scheduling apps, and the secondary profiles you use for testing, private conversations, or niche communities. If one of those pieces is compromised, the impact can spread quickly because social platforms are built to connect identities, not isolate them. That interconnectedness is useful, but it also means a weak link can become a doorway.

A useful way to map your exposure is to sort it by consequence, not by convenience. Ask which account would cause the most damage if taken over, which content would be most harmful if exposed, and which connected service would let an attacker move farther into your digital life. For an individual, the highest-risk items may be a primary email account, a phone number used for recovery, private photo archives, or message threads containing personal details. For a creator or business, the most sensitive assets may include the main brand account, admin access to a page or ad manager, customer contact lists, unpublished content, and any tool that can send messages or publish on your behalf. This kind of ranking matters because not every asset deserves the same level of attention, but the top tier almost always deserves the strongest protection.

Content deserves the same scrutiny as accounts. A post can be sensitive even if it does not look private at first glance. Draft announcements, behind-the-scenes footage, screenshots of dashboards, travel plans, client conversations, invoices, contracts, and casual photos that reveal locations or routines can all be useful to an attacker. Public content can also be sensitive when it helps establish credibility. If someone can copy your voice, reuse your images, or imitate your style, they may be able to deceive your audience without ever touching your password. That is why content mapping should include not only what you have posted, but what you have saved, scheduled, archived, or shared in closed groups. In a world where AI-generated text and media can imitate tone and appearance with increasing ease, the value of original content and the risk of misuse both rise [82][85].

Connected services often carry more risk than users expect because they sit outside the social app while still having authority over it. A third-party scheduling tool may be able to publish posts. An analytics platform may see performance data and account identifiers. A design tool may hold brand assets and login tokens. A password manager, cloud drive, or shared inbox may contain recovery paths that make account takeover easier. The more services you attach, the more important it becomes to know exactly what each one can do. Zero trust thinking is useful here: do not assume a service is safe simply because it is convenient or widely used; verify what access it has and remove anything it does not truly need [86]. This is especially important in environments where data moves through many layers and systems, because complexity itself increases risk [56][84].

One practical method is to create a simple inventory with four columns: asset, sensitivity, access path, and dependency. Under asset, list the account, content set, or service. Under sensitivity, mark whether it is low, medium, or high risk if exposed, altered, or lost. Under access path, note how it is reached: password, recovery email, phone, admin role, app token, shared login, or device session. Under dependency, write what else relies on it. For example, your main Instagram account may depend on a recovery email, an authenticator app, a cloud folder of media, and a scheduling platform. If you cannot see the chain, you cannot secure it properly. The goal is not to produce a perfect spreadsheet; it is to reveal hidden relationships before an attacker does.

Pay special attention to places where personal and business life overlap. Many people use the same phone, the same browser, the same email habits, and sometimes even the same password patterns across multiple identities. That overlap creates a single point of failure. If a personal account is weak, it can become a path into a business profile. If a business tool is compromised, it can expose personal contact information or private conversations. Digital technologies have made these relationships more data-rich and more tightly linked, which has also intensified privacy concerns and changed how people protect themselves [81]. The more your account ecosystem blends roles, the more important it is to separate what can be separated and to document what cannot.

Finally, map not only what you own but what others can do in your name. Admin roles, collaborator access, delegated publishing rights, trusted contacts, and shared device sessions can all be legitimate and still be risky. A person with too much access, or access that is no longer needed, becomes part of your security surface. Review who can post, who can approve, who can reset, and who can recover. If a service or person does not need continuing authority, remove it. If a piece of content would be damaging in the wrong hands, treat it as sensitive even before it is published. Security starts to improve when you can answer a simple question for each item: if this were lost, copied, changed, or impersonated, how far would the damage spread?

CHAPTER 3

Chapter 3: Building a Security-First Social Media Mindset

Security on social media is not built only through settings and tools; it is shaped by the habits that govern what you notice, what you ignore, and how quickly you act when something feels off. A security-first mindset treats each post, follow request, login prompt, and reply as part of a larger pattern rather than a one-time decision. That means learning to evaluate choices before they become problems and to make protection a normal part of using the platform instead of an emergency response after damage is done.

Thinking like an attacker to spot weak points before they are exploited

A useful security habit is to ask, "If I were trying to break into this account, what would I look for first?" That question shifts you from passive checking to active inspection. An attacker usually does not begin with a dramatic exploit. They begin with convenience. They look for the easiest path, the least resistance, and the smallest mistake that opens a larger door. On social platforms, that might be a weak recovery option, a predictable posting pattern, a public email address, a reused profile photo, or a staff member who can be persuaded to click without verifying. Thinking this way does not make you paranoid. It makes you realistic.

Start by examining your profile the way a stranger would. What can be learned in less than a minute? Your name, employer, city, role, family relationships, recent travel, and preferred contact method may all be visible without any special effort. Then ask what can be inferred from the pieces that are not explicitly stated. A work schedule can be guessed from posting times. A vacation can be guessed from a sudden pause in activity. A likely password reset path can be guessed from the email address you use publicly or the phone number listed in a bio. This is how attackers work: they assemble small clues into a usable picture. That same method can be used defensively to spot what you have made too easy to assemble.

It also helps to think in terms of friction. Safe systems create little barriers that slow an attacker down. Unsafe systems remove them. If your account can be reset through a publicly known email address, if your direct messages are open to anyone, if your business page has no clear process for verifying requests, or if every linked tool shares the same login path, then you have reduced the attacker's workload. A strong defense adds friction at the points where misuse is most likely. That may mean limiting who can contact you, reducing what is visible to non-followers, separating personal and business contact methods, or requiring a second approval step before a high-impact action is taken.

One of the most valuable attacker questions is, "What would I do after I got in?" Many people focus only on the login screen, but an intruder often uses access as a starting point, not an end goal. They may change recovery details, observe private conversations, harvest contacts, post a link to spread the compromise, or impersonate the account in a way that looks ordinary enough to pass initial scrutiny. This is why you should inspect not only the front door but the rooms behind it. Look at what an attacker could alter quietly: profile name, bio, contact links, pinned posts, story highlights, connected apps, admin roles, and recovery settings. The first sign of trouble is not always a locked-out account. Sometimes it is a subtle change that makes the account easier to use later for fraud or impersonation.

Another useful angle is to ask where trust is being borrowed. Social media attacks often succeed because the message comes from a familiar source: a known friend, a partner account, a brand you follow, or a platform-branded notification. Attackers exploit the trust people already have in the relationship, not just in the technology. So when you review your own presence, look for places where your identity could be used to lend credibility to someone else's scam, or where someone else's identity could be used to reach you. A compromised friend account may send a request that feels harmless. A fake collaborator may ask for a file, a code, or a login. A copied brand voice may ask followers to "confirm" something urgent. The weakness is not just technical. It is social.

This is also why routine matters. A one-time audit is helpful, but attackers adapt, and so do the systems around you. New followers arrive, new apps get connected, settings change, and old assumptions become outdated. Build the habit of looking for weak points the way an adversary would look for them: where is the easiest entry, the fastest payoff, the least monitored path, and the most believable deception? When you can answer those questions before someone else does, you are no longer waiting for an incident to reveal your blind spots. You are identifying them while they are still fixable.

The role of routine, discipline, and friction in safer online behavior

The safest online behavior is rarely the result of a single dramatic decision. It usually comes from small, repeated choices made before you are tired, distracted, rushed, or emotionally engaged. That is why routine matters. When checking account security becomes a normal part of using social media, you rely less on memory and more on pattern. A routine does not make a person invulnerable, but it does reduce the number of moments when an attacker can exploit a lapse in attention. In practice, this means deciding in advance when you will review login alerts, when you will clean up old connections, and when you will pause to verify a request before answering it.

Discipline is what keeps those routines from becoming optional. On social platforms, many risky actions happen because a moment feels convenient: a quick tap to approve a login, a fast response to a direct message, a reused password because it is easier, a public post because it is faster than checking the audience setting. Discipline interrupts that convenience. It creates a standard that applies even when the platform encourages speed. This is especially important because social media systems are built to reward immediacy. Notifications, streaks, trending topics, and urgent-looking messages all push users toward reflexive behavior. A disciplined user recognizes that not every prompt deserves an immediate response.

Friction is often misunderstood as a problem to remove, but in security it can be a protective feature. A little friction slows down impulsive actions long enough for judgment to catch up. For example, requiring a password manager to fill credentials, using multi-factor authentication, or forcing yourself to verify a sender through a second channel all add steps. Those steps may feel inconvenient in the moment, but they make it harder for an attacker to succeed through speed or pressure. Security researchers and business practitioners often emphasize that effective control depends on how people actually behave in context, not just on the rule itself [111][112]. If a safeguard is too easy to bypass, people will bypass it. If it creates a brief pause at the right moment, it can change the outcome.

The goal is not to make social media miserable or unusable. It is to place friction where it protects you and remove friction where it helps you stay consistent. A good example is the difference between posting and responding. Posting can remain relatively easy if your content rules are clear. Responding to unexpected requests, however, should be slower by design. You may decide that any request involving money, account access, brand partnerships, or urgent help must be verified outside the platform before you act. That rule does not eliminate all risk, but it creates a speed bump at the exact point where manipulation is most likely. In a digital environment where pressure and urgency are common tactics, that pause is valuable.

Routine also protects against the false confidence that comes from "I would notice if something were wrong." Most breaches and scams succeed because the target is busy, not because the target is careless all the time. A person who checks security only after something seems suspicious is already behind. A person who reviews active sessions, connected apps, and recovery settings on a schedule is less dependent on intuition. The same logic applies to content and communication habits. If you regularly ask whether a post reveals location, routine, or relationship clues, you are less likely to publish something that creates a future problem. Repetition builds judgment by making the review process familiar.

For small teams, creators, and businesses, routine and discipline also reduce inconsistency. One person may be careful while another is rushed. One assistant may know the rules while another improvises. A shared standard makes the account less dependent on individual mood or experience. That is one reason structured cybersecurity programs work better than informal "be careful" advice [110]. The more a team can rely on predictable behavior, the less room there is for accidental exposure. This can be as simple as agreeing that no one approves login prompts without confirmation, no one answers support requests from unverified accounts, and no one changes profile details without logging the change somewhere visible to the team.

Friction should also be used to protect your attention. Social media safety fails when every request feels equally important. If your process treats all messages as urgent, you will eventually make a mistake. If, instead, you build a habit of slowing down for the kinds of interactions most likely to be abused, you preserve your judgment for the moments that matter. That might mean checking the profile history of a new "partner," waiting before clicking a link in a direct message, or requiring a second review before changing a public-facing bio. These are not signs of paranoia. They are signs that you understand how digital pressure works.

Over time, safer behavior becomes less about self-control in the moment and more about designing conditions that support good choices. Routine keeps the important checks from being forgotten. Discipline keeps convenience from overruling caution. Friction gives you time to think before you act. Together, they turn security from an occasional reaction into an ordinary part of how you use social media.

Balancing visibility and privacy without disappearing from the platform

Visibility and privacy are not opposites on social media. If you treat them that way, you end up with a false choice: either post freely and expose too much, or lock everything down so tightly that the account stops working for its purpose. A better approach is to decide what kind of visibility you actually need, then build privacy boundaries around it. Most people do not need to be invisible. They need to be reachable, credible, and selective about what is public. That distinction matters because attackers often benefit when users either overshare without thinking or overcorrect by making every interaction feel suspicious and closed off.

The first question is not “How private can I make this?” but “Who needs to see this, and why?” A creator may need public posts to attract an audience, a small business may need open contact details for customers, and an individual may want a public profile for professional networking. None of those goals require full exposure. You can keep a public-facing presence while still limiting what strangers can learn from it. The key is to separate discoverability from intimacy. Being discoverable means people can find you and understand the basic purpose of your account. Being intimate means they can infer your routines, relationships, location habits, or private life. The first is often necessary. The second is usually optional.

That separation starts with content choices. Public posts should be written as if they may be seen by a broad, mixed audience that includes customers, coworkers, competitors, strangers, and automated tools. If a post would be embarrassing, revealing, or easily misused in the wrong hands, it probably belongs in a smaller audience or not online at all. This does not mean you must post bland, lifeless content. It means you should avoid turning routine details into a public record. A photo of a product launch is one thing; a photo that reveals the exact room, time, badge, or travel pattern behind it is another. A message of support for a cause is one thing; a real-time update that places you at a sensitive event with identifiable companions is another. Research on how digital spaces shape behavior and influence shows that what is visible can be interpreted and repurposed in ways users do not always anticipate [10][117].

It also helps to think in layers. Your profile does not need to say everything in the same place. The bio can explain what you do without listing your home city, school, or family details. The profile photo can be recognizable without being a high-resolution image that makes it easy to copy or reuse. Posts can show work, interests, and expertise without revealing schedules, travel plans, or live location clues. Comments can be helpful without being overly personal. If you run a business or public brand, create a boundary between the account that attracts attention and the information that confirms trust. People should be able to understand who you are, but they should not be able to reconstruct your life from the account alone.

Another useful habit is to reduce the amount of accidental context your account gives away. Even when a post seems harmless, the combination of timing, background details, tagged names, and repeated habits can expose more than the content itself. That is why "I only post public information" is not a sufficient privacy strategy. Public information becomes sensitive when it is aggregated, repeated, and tied to your identity. A modest amount of discipline around posting times, location tags, friend tags, and recurring personal routines can make a large difference. This is especially important for people who work in public-facing roles, manage community groups, or operate in environments where harassment, stalking, or targeted scams are realistic concerns. Studies of privacy behavior across different user groups show that vulnerability is often shaped by context and routine, not just by age or technical skill [118].

Selective engagement matters just as much as selective posting. You do not have to reply to every message, accept every follow request, or comment on every issue to remain active. In fact, a measured response pattern often looks more trustworthy than a frantic one. Scammers and impersonators frequently exploit urgency and constant availability, assuming that a visible account will also be a reactive one. Setting expectations helps: use clear contact channels, define when you respond, and reserve private communication for verified relationships. If your account is public, let the public part serve its purpose while keeping sensitive discussions off the open feed. That approach preserves accessibility without turning your profile into an invitation for pressure or manipulation.

There is also a psychological side to this balance. People often swing between two extremes: either they share too much because they want connection, or they become so cautious that they stop participating altogether. Neither extreme is ideal. A sustainable privacy posture is one that you can maintain without resentment. If the rules are so strict that you constantly feel constrained, you will eventually ignore them. If the rules are so loose that you feel exposed, you will eventually withdraw. The goal is a practical middle ground: enough openness to be present, enough restraint to stay in control. That middle ground is not static. It changes with your role, your audience, and the sensitivity of what you are doing at any given time. A personal account, a creator account, and a business account may each need a different balance, but all three benefit from the same principle: let the platform show what it must, and no more than necessary.

Creating personal rules for posting, connecting, and responding

Personal rules work best when they are simple enough to follow when you are busy, tired, or reacting quickly. Social media creates a steady stream of small decisions, and most security mistakes happen in those ordinary moments rather than during a dramatic breach. Research on privacy and security decision-making shows that people often struggle when choices are frequent, complex, and time-sensitive, which is exactly why a personal code is useful [122]. Instead of trying to evaluate every post, request, or reply from scratch, you set a few standards in advance and let those standards do the work for you.

A good posting rule starts with one question: Would I still want this visible if it were shared beyond the audience I intended? That question is not about paranoia; it is about recognizing how easily context changes online. A post meant for friends can be copied, screenshotted, forwarded, or surfaced later in a different setting. Build a habit of checking whether the content reveals anything you would not want tied to your name, your workplace, your family, your travel pattern, or your current location. If a post includes a face, a place, a schedule, a document, a badge, a child, or a screen in the background, slow down and decide whether the benefit of posting outweighs the exposure. If you are managing a public-facing brand, apply the same discipline to drafts, behind-the-scenes content, and casual updates, because "informal" still becomes part of your public record once it is published.

It also helps to define what is never posted, no matter how harmless it seems in the moment. Many people do better with a short list than with broad principles. For example: no live location from home or work; no travel announcements until after returning; no images that expose account details, shipping labels, tickets, or internal messages; no screenshots that include private conversations unless everyone involved has agreed; no reposting of sensitive family or business information without permission. These rules reduce the need for constant judgment. They also protect you from the temptation to share while emotional, when judgment is usually weaker and the audience feels closer than it really is. The goal is not to remove personality from your account. The goal is to keep your personality from becoming a map.

Your rules for connecting should be just as deliberate. Every follow request, friend request, collaboration pitch, and new message is a trust decision, even if it feels casual. Decide in advance what counts as enough verification before you connect with someone, especially if they ask for access, information, introductions, or a move to another platform.

If an account is new, vague, oddly polished, or inconsistent with the person it claims to represent, treat that as a reason to verify rather than a reason to engage quickly. When possible, confirm identity through a second channel you already trust. For business accounts, it may be worth requiring that partnership requests come from an official domain or a documented contact path rather than from a direct message alone. The point is to make access earned, not assumed.

A useful rule here is to separate visibility from intimacy. Not everyone who can view your content should be able to reach you in the same way, and not everyone who can contact you should be able to influence your decisions. That means limiting who can DM you, who can tag you, who can add you to groups, and who can see the more personal parts of your profile. It also means being careful with mutual connections, because attackers often use familiar names to lower your guard. If someone pressures you to "move fast," "keep it private," or "skip the formalities," that pressure itself is information. A legitimate person can usually tolerate a normal verification process.

Rules for responding matter because attackers often rely on urgency, embarrassment, or curiosity to push you into a bad choice. Before replying to a message that asks for money, credentials, codes, links, or a quick favor, pause and ask whether the request makes sense in context. If it does not, do not improvise. Use a standard response such as "I'll verify this another way" or "Please send that through the official channel." For public comments, avoid being drawn into arguments, bait, or fake support threads that try to move the conversation into private messages. In many cases, the safest response is no response at all until you have checked the account, the request, and the surrounding context. AI-assisted scams and impersonation attempts are making deceptive messages more convincing and more personalized, which raises the value of a consistent response rule rather than a case-by-case emotional reaction [123][61].

Your response rules should also cover what you never disclose in the moment. Do not share verification codes, backup codes, passwords, payment details, or account recovery information in a reply, even if the message sounds official. Do not confirm sensitive facts just because someone already knows a few of them. Do not let a flattering message, an urgent complaint, or a public accusation pull you into revealing more than you intended. If you are a creator or business owner, create a separate rule for public correction: acknowledge the issue briefly, move the conversation to a secure channel if needed, and avoid oversharing internal details before you know what happened. A calm, prewritten approach protects both your account and your credibility.

The most effective personal rules are the ones you can actually remember. Keep them short, concrete, and visible enough to use. A good standard might be: pause before posting, verify before connecting, and never respond under pressure. Another might be: if it affects safety, money, access, or reputation, slow down and check it twice. These rules do not replace settings, authentication, or platform controls. They support them by giving you a consistent way to act when the situation is noisy, fast, or uncertain.

CHAPTER 4

Chapter 4: Locking Down Accounts Before Trouble Starts

Before you can make a social account safer, you have to treat access itself as a security layer, not just a convenience. A locked-down profile is not built after a warning sign appears; it is prepared in advance so that a stolen password, a rushed click, or a compromised device does not immediately turn into a full takeover. That preparation begins with the basics that are easy to postpone and easy to regret later: how credentials are stored, how sign-in is confirmed, how control is regained if something breaks, and how quietly attached services can widen the risk surface.

Strong password practices and password manager use across platforms

Passwords are still the first gate most platforms rely on, which is why weak or repeated credentials remain one of the fastest ways into a social account. A strong password is not just long; it is also difficult to guess, difficult to reuse, and difficult to connect to anything else about you. That means avoiding names, birthdays, pet names, sports teams, favorite phrases, keyboard patterns, and any variation that can be assembled from your public profile. Attackers routinely test those patterns because they are easy to predict and often surprisingly effective. The safest approach is to treat each platform as if it needs a password that has no relationship to any other account, any personal detail, or any memory shortcut you could accidentally repeat elsewhere.

The easiest way to create that standard is to stop trying to invent passwords from scratch every time. A password manager lets you generate long, unique credentials for each platform and store them in an encrypted vault instead of in your head or in a notes app. That matters because the real problem is not only forgetting a password; it is the pressure to simplify one password so it can be reused everywhere. Once a password manager is in place, the goal becomes consistency: every social account gets its own unique password, and that password is never copied to another service. This approach fits the broader security principle of limiting unnecessary trust and reducing the blast radius when one account is exposed [86].

When choosing a password manager, look for one that works across the devices and browsers you actually use. If you post from a phone, review messages on a tablet, and manage a business account from a laptop, the tool should follow you without creating a new source of friction. It should also support strong local device protection, such as a master password, biometric unlock where appropriate, and automatic locking after inactivity. The master password deserves special care because it becomes the key to everything else. Make it long, unique, and memorable enough that you do not need to write it down in an obvious place. If the manager offers a recovery method, understand it before you need it, because a rushed setup often leads to weak backup choices later.

For social media use, the manager should also help you separate personal, creator, and business access. That means storing credentials in distinct vaults or folders when the tool supports it, and limiting who can see shared logins if you work with a team. A shared business account should not be handled like a family streaming login. Access should be granted only to the people who need it, and removed promptly when roles change. This kind of controlled access reflects a broader zero-trust mindset: do not assume a login is safe simply because it belongs to someone you know [86]. Even trusted collaborators can lose devices, leave a company, or make mistakes under pressure.

One common mistake is to let the password manager do all the work while the underlying habits stay the same. If you save a weak password once and then reuse it through autofill, the tool has preserved convenience but not security. Use the manager to replace weak credentials, not to archive them. After a password is changed, update it everywhere the account is connected: mobile app, desktop browser, scheduling tool, ad dashboard, or creator marketplace. If a platform offers a sign-in history, review it after the change so you can confirm that the new credential is being used only where expected. This is especially important for accounts tied to audience trust, because a hidden compromise can continue even after the visible password has been replaced.

It is also wise to keep the password manager itself as simple as possible. Do not store unrelated sensitive material in the same vault unless the tool is designed for that purpose and you have a clear reason to do so. The more clutter a vault contains, the harder it becomes to audit what matters. Periodically review the saved logins and delete old accounts you no longer use. Old platform accounts, test profiles, and dormant services are easy to forget, but they can still become entry points if they were protected with weak or recycled passwords. Research on digital systems consistently shows that privacy and trust are shaped by how data and access are managed over time, not just at the moment of sign-up [81].

Finally, make password recovery part of the password plan. A strong password is only useful if you can still regain access when a device is lost, a browser is reset, or a login is challenged. Store recovery codes in a secure place, keep your recovery email account equally protected, and avoid relying on text-only methods when a stronger option is available. For any account that matters to your identity, audience, or business, the password manager should be treated as the control center for access, not as a convenience add-on. The objective is not to make login harder for you; it is to make unauthorized access harder for everyone else.

Multi-factor authentication options and how to choose the safest method

Multi-factor authentication works best when it adds resistance without making recovery so difficult that you lock yourself out under pressure. The basic idea is simple: a password alone is not enough, so a second factor is required before access is granted. In practice, that second factor can take several forms, and the safest choice is not always the one that feels most familiar. The question is not just whether a platform offers MFA, but which method gives you the strongest protection against the attacks most likely to target a social account.

The main options usually fall into four categories. The first is SMS codes sent to your phone. This is better than no second factor at all, but it is the weakest common option because phone numbers can be intercepted, redirected, or abused through account recovery fraud. The second is app-based codes from an authenticator app, which generates short-lived codes on your device. This is generally stronger than SMS because the code is not traveling through the mobile network. The third is push-based approval, where you receive a prompt asking you to tap "approve" or "deny." This can be convenient, but it is only as safe as the process that triggers the prompt, and repeated prompts can train people to approve without thinking. The fourth is a hardware security key, a physical device that must be present to complete login. For many users, this is the strongest available option because it resists remote interception and many phishing attempts.

If you want the safest practical method, start by looking for phishing resistance. That matters because social media accounts are often targeted through convincing login pages, fake support messages, and urgent requests that try to capture both password and second factor in one step. A code sent by text or generated by an app can still be stolen if you enter it into a fake page. A hardware key, by contrast, verifies the site itself as part of the sign-in process, which makes it much harder for a fake login page to succeed. This is why security guidance in many environments treats hardware-based authentication as the strongest everyday option for high-value accounts. It is not perfect, but it raises the bar in a way that is especially useful for creators, business pages, and personal accounts tied to reputation or revenue.

That said, the safest method on paper is not always the safest method for your routine. If you travel often, switch devices, share access with a team, or rely on a platform for daily work, you need a method you can actually use consistently. An authenticator app is often the best balance for individual users because it is stronger than SMS, relatively easy to set up, and does not depend on your phone number being secure. A hardware key is a better choice for accounts that would be especially damaging to lose, but you should treat it as part of a system, not a single object. That means having a backup key stored securely, knowing which devices support it, and confirming that the platform lets you recover access without weakening your protection.

Push-based approval deserves special caution. It can be useful when paired with a number-matching prompt or a device-bound approval process, but it becomes risky if it is used as a simple yes-or-no tap. Attackers can bombard users with repeated prompts until one is approved, especially when the victim is distracted or assumes the request is legitimate. If you use push notifications, make it a rule never to approve a prompt unless you personally initiated the login and can verify the context. If the platform allows only basic push approval and no stronger option, consider whether an authenticator app or security key is available instead.

A good selection process is to ask four questions. First, what is the account worth to an attacker? An account with a large audience, payment access, or brand authority deserves the strongest method available. Second, what kind of attack is most likely? If phishing is the main concern, choose a phishing-resistant option when possible. Third, what will happen if you lose the device or key? The more important the account, the more carefully you need backup codes and recovery methods. Fourth, what can you maintain without making mistakes? The safest method is the one you will keep enabled, keep backed up, and keep using correctly. Research on account recovery and 2FA adoption shows that users often enroll in second-factor protection but do not always manage the recovery side well, which can create a different kind of risk [149]. In other words, the protection is only as strong as the way you prepare for loss, replacement, or emergency access.

For most readers, the decision can be made in a practical order. If a hardware security key is supported and you can keep a backup key in a secure place, use it for the most important accounts. If not, use an authenticator app rather than SMS whenever possible. Reserve text-message codes for accounts with lower risk or for services that offer no better choice. Avoid treating any one method as a set-it-and-forget-it solution. The safest setup is the one that combines a strong second factor with clear recovery planning, because an account you cannot regain is not truly secure either.

Recovery settings, backup codes, and trusted contact planning

Recovery features are only useful if they are set up before you need them. On social platforms, the most common mistake is assuming that a password reset link will be enough to restore access later. In reality, recovery is a separate security path, and if that path is weak, stale, or controlled by the wrong person, it can become the easiest way to lose an account. A determined attacker may not need to defeat your password at all if they can intercept a code, access your recovery email, or manipulate the platform into trusting the wrong contact information. That is why recovery settings deserve the same attention as the login itself.

Start by checking every account you care about and asking a simple question: if I lost access today, what would the platform use to verify me? The answer may be a phone number, an email address, an authenticator app, security questions, backup codes, or a trusted contact feature. Each of those options should be current, private, and reachable by you alone. A recovery email that is also used for newsletters, shopping, or old signups creates unnecessary exposure. A phone number that is shared widely or tied to an old device can become a weak point if the number is ported, recycled, or accessed by someone else. Good recovery planning is less about adding every possible option and more about making sure the options you keep are the right ones.

Backup codes are especially important because they often become the last reliable way back into an account after a device change, app failure, or authentication problem. Treat them like keys, not convenience text. If a platform gives you a set of one-time codes, save them in a secure place that is separate from the device you use every day. A password manager is usually a better home than a screenshot in your photo gallery or a note app synced across multiple devices. If you print them, store the paper somewhere private and protected from casual access. The goal is to make the codes available when you are locked out, but not available to anyone who gains brief access to your phone, laptop, or shared cloud storage.

It is also worth testing whether your backup method actually works before you depend on it. Many people enable recovery features and never verify them again. That can leave them with expired codes, an old email address, or a trusted device that no longer exists. Review recovery settings after changing phones, email providers, business roles, or SIM cards. If a platform lets you generate new backup codes, replace the old set and remove any copies you no longer need. If you suspect a code may have been exposed, assume it is compromised and regenerate the set immediately. Recovery should be treated as a living part of account security, not a one-time setup task.

Trusted contact planning requires the same discipline. Some platforms allow you to designate people who can help confirm your identity or assist in recovery. That feature can be useful, but only if the people you choose are trustworthy, reachable, and unlikely to be manipulated through your public profile. Pick contacts who understand that helping you recover an account is a responsibility, not a casual favor. They should know not to share codes, not to approve requests they do not recognize, and not to act based on messages that merely appear urgent. If you use trusted contacts for a business or creator account, separate personal relationships from operational roles whenever possible so a social dispute or personal emergency does not become a security failure.

The planning step matters because attackers often target the recovery process through social pressure rather than technical skill. They may impersonate you, contact a trusted person, or exploit the fact that people want to be helpful when they think an account is in distress. That is why your contacts need a clear rule: they should only respond to requests through a prearranged verification method you define in advance. For example, you might agree that any recovery help must be confirmed by a phone call, a message from a known number, or a second channel that is not tied to the compromised platform. Without that rule, the most security-minded friend or colleague can still become the weak link.

A practical recovery plan should fit on one page and be easy to update. At minimum, it should identify the primary recovery email, the backup email if one exists, where backup codes are stored, which trusted contacts are selected, and how you will confirm a real recovery request. Keep that plan private, but make sure the people involved understand only what they need to know. For business accounts, it helps to document who owns recovery access, who can approve changes, and what happens if a staff member leaves or a device is lost. Research on cyber incidents consistently shows that weak process and poor access control can be as damaging as technical flaws [151][63]. Recovery planning is one of the clearest places where process protects the account before a crisis starts.

Finally, remember that recovery settings are not only for emergencies. They are part of routine account hygiene. Review them when you update passwords, change devices, add new team members, or notice unusual login activity. If a platform offers recovery alerts, turn them on. If it offers a way to view or change trusted contacts, check that list periodically. The best recovery plan is the one you could use under stress without guessing, improvising, or relying on memory.

Reviewing login alerts, active sessions, and connected apps regularly

Login alerts are only useful if you treat them as signals, not background noise. A new sign-in notification can mean you logged in from a different device, but it can also mean someone else is trying to get in, or already has. The habit to build is simple: when an alert arrives, pause and verify the context immediately. Ask whether the location, device type, browser, and time make sense. If the alert does not match your own activity, do not dismiss it and move on. Open the platform through your normal route, review the security page, and confirm whether the event is legitimate. Social engineering often succeeds because people are conditioned to react quickly and trust messages that look routine [156]. Login alerts deserve the opposite response: deliberate checking before any action.

Many platforms now show a list of recent sign-ins, including approximate location, device model, operating system, and sign-in time. That record is valuable because it lets you compare normal behavior against unfamiliar access. You are not looking for perfection; location data can be imprecise, and mobile networks sometimes create odd results. What matters is pattern recognition. If your account normally signs in from one city and suddenly shows repeated access from another region, or if you see logins at hours when you were asleep, that is worth investigating. The same is true if the device list shows hardware you do not own or a browser you never use. Attackers often test access in small steps before they attempt a larger takeover, so early review can reveal trouble while it is still contained.

Active sessions deserve the same attention because a valid login can remain open long after the original sign-in. Someone who has accessed your account from a borrowed device, a shared computer, or a compromised phone may still be present even after the password changes if the platform has not fully revoked the session. That is why the session list should be checked regularly, not only after a problem. Look for unfamiliar devices, strange locations, or sessions that have been active far longer than expected. If the platform gives you the option to log out of individual sessions or all sessions at once, use it when you see anything suspicious. This is one of the few security actions that can remove an intruder without requiring you to guess how they got in.

For people who manage business or creator accounts, session review should be even more disciplined because access often spreads across more than one person or device. A marketing assistant may use one login, a contractor another, and a phone app another still. Over time, that convenience can turn into confusion. Someone leaves a project, changes roles, or stops using an old phone, and the account still remembers them. That lingering access is a security gap as much as a technical one. Periodic session review forces you to answer a practical question: who should still be able to act as this account today? If the answer is unclear, the account is carrying unnecessary risk.

Connected apps are another place where forgotten access quietly accumulates. Social platforms frequently allow third-party tools to post on your behalf, read profile information, manage pages, pull analytics, or connect to cloud storage and scheduling systems. Those permissions are often granted during a busy moment, then never revisited. The problem is not only malicious software; it is also legitimate tools that no longer need the access they once had. A scheduling app you stopped using six months ago, a quiz tool from a campaign you forgot about, or a browser extension installed for one project can remain linked indefinitely. Each connection expands the number of places an attacker might exploit if that service is compromised [155]. If a connected app does not serve a current need, remove it.

When reviewing connected apps, do not stop at the name of the service. Open the permission details and check what the app can actually do. Some tools request broad access that goes far beyond what their function requires. A simple analytics add-on may have permission to read messages, manage content, or access profile data it does not need. That mismatch is a warning sign. It is also worth checking whether the app is associated with a company you recognize, whether it still has an active support page, and whether its privacy policy or security page has changed in a way that affects your risk. Usable security depends on making these checks practical enough to repeat, which is why the review should be short, specific, and scheduled rather than vague and occasional [50].

A good routine is to combine all three checks into one brief security pass. Review login alerts for anything unfamiliar, scan active sessions for devices that should not still be there, and audit connected apps for permissions you no longer need. If you find something suspicious, act in order: end the session, change the password if needed, confirm multi-factor authentication is still active, and remove any app you do not trust. If the platform offers a “log out of all devices” option, use it after a confirmed compromise or when you cannot confidently identify every active session. The goal is not to become obsessed with every technical detail. It is to make sure that access to your account is visible enough that you can notice when it stops being yours alone.

CHAPTER 5

Chapter 5: Privacy Settings That Actually Matter

Privacy settings are where the abstract idea of “being careful” becomes an operational choice. They determine who can see your activity, how easily your profile can be found, and how much of your presence is exposed by default when you post, interact, or connect with others. For most people, the goal is not to hide completely; it is to reduce unnecessary exposure so the account reflects your intended audience instead of the platform’s default assumptions. That means treating privacy as a control surface, not a single switch. Some settings matter far more than others, and a few small changes can sharply reduce the amount of information an outsider can gather from ordinary use.

Audience controls for posts, stories, comments, and profile visibility

Audience controls are most effective when you treat them as separate decisions instead of one broad privacy choice. A post, a story, a comment, and a profile all serve different purposes, and each one can expose different information to different people. The safest approach is to decide, in advance, who needs to see what. That means not relying on the platform’s default audience, which is often broader than necessary, and not assuming that “followers” or “friends” are automatically a safe group. In practice, audience control is about matching visibility to purpose: public when reach matters, limited when context matters, and restricted when the content reveals more than it should.

For regular posts, the main question is whether the content is meant to be discoverable by strangers or only by a defined circle. Public posts can be useful for branding, outreach, and search visibility, but they also create permanent, reusable material for anyone who wants to map your habits, voice, or relationships. If a post includes location cues, family details, business routines, internal events, or anything that could be repurposed in a scam, limit the audience before publishing. Many platforms let you choose between public, followers-only, friends-only, custom lists, or close-friends-style groups. Use the narrowest setting that still fits the purpose of the post. If you are posting on behalf of a business, separate promotional content from internal updates so that public visibility does not accidentally become the default for everything.

Stories deserve even more discipline because they feel temporary, which often makes people overshare. The short lifespan of a story does not make it low risk; it often makes it easier to post without reflection. Stories can reveal where you are, who you are with, what time you are active, and what routines repeat from day to day. A viewer does not need a long archive if they can collect enough detail over a week. Restrict story audiences to people who genuinely need that level of access, and use exclusion features when a particular group should not see certain content. If you maintain both personal and public-facing accounts, do not assume that a story posted for one audience will stay in that lane unless the settings clearly enforce it. For creators and small businesses, it is especially important to keep behind-the-scenes content separate from anything that could expose travel plans, staffing patterns, or sensitive operational details.

Comments are another area where audience control often gets overlooked because the focus stays on what you publish, not on what others can attach to it. Yet comments can reveal just as much as posts, especially when they expose your availability, your location, your relationships, or your emotional state. Restrict who can comment on posts and stories when the account attracts spam, impersonation, or harassment. If the platform allows comment filters, keyword blocks, or approval controls, use them. This is not only about reducing abuse; it is also about preventing strangers from using your public content as a place to bait you into a response. A hostile comment thread can draw attention to a post you would rather keep low-profile, and a fake support reply can mislead followers into trusting the wrong account. On public-facing profiles, it is often wise to allow comments only where engagement is worth the risk and to disable them where the content is informational rather than conversational.

Profile visibility is the foundation underneath all of these settings. Even if your posts are limited, a profile can still reveal enough to identify you, locate you, or target you. Review what is visible to people who are not approved connections: your bio, profile photo, cover image, email address, phone number, website, workplace, school, birthday, pronouns, and any link that points to another account or service. Limit discovery settings so that your profile cannot be found too easily through phone number or email lookup unless that discoverability is intentional. If the platform allows you to hide your friend list, followers, or mutual connections, consider whether those lists create unnecessary exposure. In many cases, the profile itself should answer only the question “Is this the right account?” and not “What else can I learn from this person right now?”

A useful habit is to test your own account as if you were an outsider. Open the profile from a logged-out view, a secondary account, or a trusted device that is not connected to your main session. Look at each element separately: what appears on the profile page, what a stranger can learn from a first post, what a viewer can infer from story highlights, and what shows up in comment threads. This kind of review often reveals settings that technically exist but are not working together. A private post can still be linked from a public profile. A restricted story can still be screenshot by someone you allowed in. A hidden friend list may still be implied by visible interactions. The point is not to eliminate all exposure; it is to make exposure deliberate.

The safest audience strategy is usually layered. Keep the profile itself as sparse as possible, keep public content purposeful, and reserve the most personal material for the smallest audience that genuinely needs it. If a setting is confusing, default to narrower access until you can verify how it behaves. Social platforms are designed to encourage sharing, and their interface often makes broad visibility feel normal. Your job is to resist that drift and keep the audience attached to each post, story, comment, and profile element aligned with the real security value of the content.

Location sharing, tagging permissions, and discovery settings

Location sharing is one of the easiest settings to overlook because it often appears harmless in isolation. A single check-in, a live map feature, or a geotag on a photo can seem useful, even routine. The problem is that location data becomes more revealing when it is repeated over time. One post may tell someone where you are. A pattern of posts can tell them where you live, where you work, when you travel, when your home is empty, and which places you visit often. That is why location controls should be treated as a boundary, not a convenience setting. If the platform offers precise location tagging, automatic geotagging, or background location access, disable anything you do not actively need. If you do need to share a location for a specific event or promotion, make it deliberate, temporary, and limited to the smallest audience possible.

The safest default is usually to remove location metadata before posting, especially for personal content, family photos, and anything that could reveal routine. Many users do not realize that a picture taken at home, at a child's school event, or at a client site can contain more information than the image itself. Even when the platform strips some metadata on upload, you should not assume every app or workflow does the same. If you manage social content for a business, build a simple rule: location is shared only when it serves a clear purpose. A coffee shop can post from its storefront; a consultant does not need to announce a hotel lobby, home office, or travel schedule. The less precise the location, the harder it is for an outsider to map your movements.

Tagging permissions deserve the same level of attention because tags let other people attach your name to content you did not publish. That can be useful for visibility, but it can also create exposure you never intended. A tagged photo may reveal where you were, who you were with, what you wore, what device or equipment you used, or what event you attended. For creators and small businesses, tags can also be used to pull an account into spammy promotions, fake giveaways, or misleading posts that borrow credibility from your name. Review whether tags require approval before appearing on your profile, and if the platform allows it, turn on pre-approval for photos, mentions, and tags. This does not stop people from posting about you, but it does prevent those posts from automatically becoming part of your public identity.

It is also worth separating helpful tagging from risky tagging. A business may want customers to tag a storefront or a product, and an influencer may want community posts to surface in a campaign. The key is to define what belongs on your profile and what does not. If a tag is relevant but the post is low quality, misleading, or too revealing, you can often remove the tag without creating conflict. If a tag repeatedly exposes your location, your family, or your schedule, block the source rather than treating it as a one-time annoyance. The goal is not to reject every mention. It is to prevent other people from using your profile as an attachment point for information you did not choose to publish.

Discovery settings control how easily strangers can find you in the first place. These settings often determine whether your account can be located by phone number, email address, search engines, mutual connections, or suggested-friend systems. That sounds convenient, and sometimes it is. But convenience also broadens the net for impersonators, scammers, and data harvesters. If you use social media for a business or public-facing brand, you may want some discoverability. If you use it for personal communication, private networking, or limited audience sharing, you may want much less. Review whether your profile can be found through contact information, whether search engines can index your profile, and whether the platform recommends your account to people based on imported contacts or shared networks. Disable the pathways you do not need.

This is especially important when your account contains a real name, a recognizable face, or a role that could be impersonated. A person who can easily find your profile can also more easily copy it, scrape it, or use it as a source of context for a fake message. Zero-trust thinking is useful here: do not assume that because a platform is popular, its discovery defaults are aligned with your interests [86]. Ask whether each discovery path helps the right people reach you or simply makes you easier to map. If a setting makes you more visible to strangers but does nothing for your actual goals, it is usually an unnecessary exposure.

The practical test is simple: if someone knew only your name, your phone number, or your email address, how much of your account could they uncover? If the answer is "too much," tighten the settings around location, tagging, and discovery together rather than one at a time. These controls reinforce one another. Limiting location reduces the value of tags. Limiting tags reduces the impact of being discovered. Limiting discovery reduces the number of people who can use both against you. For most users, the right balance is not maximum privacy; it is controlled visibility. You want people who already belong in your audience to find you, while making it much harder for strangers to trace your movements, attach themselves to your content, or map your profile through the platform's default assumptions.

Limiting data collection, ad personalization, and third-party access

Most platforms give you a choice between convenience and control, but the default settings usually favor collecting more information than you strictly need to share. That collection can include your activity history, device identifiers, ad interactions, contact syncing, inferred interests, and the relationships built from those signals. The important point is not that every platform is secretly doing the same thing in the same way; it is that data collection is often broader than the user expects, and the settings that limit it are usually scattered across several menus. If you do nothing, the platform will often assume that broader collection is acceptable.

The first step is to separate what helps the service function from what mainly helps it profile you. Some data use is operational: remembering that you are signed in, keeping your session active, preventing abuse, or showing you content in the language you selected. Other data use is more commercial: building an ad profile, measuring engagement, linking your activity across apps or devices, and predicting what you are likely to click next. Those functions are not always visible to the user, but privacy research consistently shows that people are more protective once they understand how much data-driven personalization shapes the experience [81].

Ad personalization is usually built from a combination of declared information and inferred behavior. Declared information includes the age, location, interests, or workplace details you enter yourself. Inferred behavior is drawn from what you view, follow, linger on, search for, and interact with over time. That means even careful users can still feed the advertising system through ordinary use. You may never post your shopping preferences directly, but repeated engagement with certain pages, creators, or topics can still be enough to create a usable profile. The practical goal is not to eliminate every signal; it is to reduce the amount of unnecessary profiling tied to your account.

When you review ad settings, look for controls that limit interest-based ads, cross-platform tracking, and the use of activity from other accounts or devices. If a platform lets you reset or clear an ad profile, do it. If it lets you opt out of personalized ads while still showing general ads, that is usually a worthwhile tradeoff. Also check whether the platform is using your contact information for ad matching. Email addresses and phone numbers are especially valuable because they can connect your social account to other services, even when you think those services are separate. A small reduction in matching data can make your overall profile less portable to advertisers and data brokers.

Third-party access deserves the same level of attention as the platform's own settings, because many privacy problems begin outside the main app. Connected apps may request permission to post on your behalf, read your profile, access your followers, manage pages, view analytics, or pull in contacts and media. Some of these permissions are necessary for legitimate tools, especially for businesses and creators who schedule content or measure performance. But permissions tend to accumulate. A tool that was useful six months ago may still have access long after you stopped using it. Regularly review every connected app, browser integration, and business tool, and remove anything you do not actively rely on.

It is also worth asking whether a third-party tool needs full access to do its job. In many cases, it does not. A scheduling app may need permission to publish posts, but not to read your private messages. An analytics service may need page metrics, but not your contact list. A quiz app, giveaway tool, or “free insights” service may request far more than it reasonably needs, and that is a warning sign. Data minimization is a basic privacy principle for a reason: when a service collects less, there is less to expose, misuse, or lose [171].

For small businesses and creators, the challenge is to avoid treating convenience as a blank check. Shared logins, delegated access, and marketing integrations can be practical, but they should be limited to named tools and named people. Use separate business accounts where possible, and avoid connecting every experiment, plugin, or promotional service to your primary profile. If a team member leaves, a contractor’s project ends, or a campaign wraps up, revoke access immediately instead of assuming the connection will expire on its own. The same discipline applies to customer-facing tools that sync followers, messages, or lead data into external systems. The more places your social data travels, the harder it becomes to control.

A useful habit is to audit your privacy posture from the outside in. Ask what a stranger, advertiser, or connected app can learn from your account without your direct approval. Then ask what an approved app can do if its permissions are broader than intended. This two-part review catches different risks: one is public exposure, the other is delegated exposure. Together they show why privacy settings are not just about hiding posts. They are about limiting how much of your digital behavior is harvested, repackaged, and redistributed beyond the audience you intended.

Platform-specific privacy audits for major social networks

A platform-specific privacy audit is not about clicking every menu item and hoping for the best. It is a deliberate review of how each network handles visibility, discovery, contact syncing, ad personalization, and account recovery. The reason this matters is that social platforms do not all expose information in the same way. A setting that is harmless on one service may be broad on another, and a feature that looks private in the interface may still share more than you expect through search, recommendations, or connected tools. The goal is to reduce accidental exposure without making the account unusable for the role it needs to play.

Start with the profile itself. On each major network, review what a non-follower or non-connection can see before you touch anything else: profile photo, bio, website link, contact buttons, pronouns, workplace, school, birthday, and any public highlights or pinned content. These details often seem routine, but together they can confirm identity, reveal a business relationship, or make impersonation easier. If the platform lets you separate public-facing identity from private contact information, do it. For business and creator accounts, use a public email address or contact form that does not expose your primary personal inbox. For personal accounts, remove fields you do not need to share at all. Digital technologies often create tension between convenience and privacy, and users typically respond best when the account reveals only the information needed for the intended relationship [81].

Next, inspect who can find you. Search discovery settings are easy to ignore because they do not feel as visible as posts or messages, yet they determine whether strangers can locate your account through email, phone number, external search engines, or platform suggestions. If you do not want to be found that way, turn those pathways off wherever the platform allows it. Do the same for contact syncing. Uploading your contacts may make it easier to "connect with people you know," but it also gives the platform more data about your relationships and can expose your account to suggestions you did not intend. If the service offers options to stop future syncing, delete uploaded contacts, or limit who can use your number or email to find you, use the strictest practical setting.

Then move to audience controls for content types. The mistake many users make is assuming that one privacy choice covers everything. It usually does not. Posts, stories, reels, comments, live streams, and reshared content may each have separate visibility rules. Review the default audience for new posts, the audience for past posts, and the visibility of stories or temporary content. If the platform lets you create a close friends list, custom audience, or restricted viewer group, use it for content that is personal but not fully private. On public-facing accounts, consider whether comments should be open to everyone, limited to followers, or filtered through approval. This is especially important for creators and small businesses, where open engagement can be useful but also invites spam, impersonation, and social engineering.

Location and tagging settings deserve the same attention. Disable automatic geotagging unless you have a clear reason to use it. Review whether others can tag you in posts, add you to photos, mention your account in stories, or include your location in shared content without approval. These features can seem harmless until they create a pattern. A single tagged photo may not matter, but repeated tags can reveal routines, travel, workplace habits, or family connections. If you manage a business account, limit who can tag the brand and how tagged content appears on your profile. That reduces the chance that misleading or low-quality content becomes associated with your name.

Ad and data controls are the least glamorous part of the audit, but they often have the widest privacy impact. Review whether the platform uses your activity for ad targeting, whether it can infer interests from engagement, and whether it may share data with partners or third-party services. Where possible, reduce personalization and opt out of features that rely on broad profiling. Also check connected apps, browser logins, and ad account permissions. Social platforms increasingly sit inside a larger ecosystem of cloud services, marketing tools, and device-linked data flows, which makes access control more important than surface-level privacy alone [19]. If an app no longer serves a clear purpose, remove it rather than leaving it attached "just in case."

A useful audit ends with a practical test: view your profile the way a stranger would. Log out or use a private browser window and inspect the account from the outside. Ask three questions. What can be seen immediately? What can be discovered with a few clicks? What can be inferred from patterns, recommendations, or past content? If the answers reveal more than you want, tighten the relevant setting and repeat the test. For platforms that support it, use separate audience lists or separate accounts for personal, professional, and experimental activity. That kind of partitioning is especially valuable in environments where data moves easily across services and devices, because the less a platform knows by default, the less it can expose if settings drift later [3][174].

CHAPTER 6

Chapter 6: Spotting Scams, Phishing, and Manipulation Tactics

Scams and manipulation on social media work because they borrow the platform's own habits of speed, familiarity, and casual trust. A message that arrives in the middle of an ordinary conversation can feel less like a threat than a routine interruption, which is exactly why these tactics remain effective. The goal is not only to trick someone into clicking a link or sharing a code; it is to steer attention, narrow judgment, and create enough pressure that the next action happens before verification. Research on misinformation and manipulation in digital spaces shows that these tactics often succeed by exploiting cognitive vulnerabilities and social context rather than technical weakness alone [72].

Red flags in direct messages, comments, emails, and fake support requests

Direct messages are one of the easiest places for a scam to hide because they arrive inside a conversation space that already feels personal. A message may look routine at first glance: a follower asking for help, a customer with a complaint, a brand partner with a proposal, or a platform notice that appears to fit the moment. The warning sign is not simply that the message is unsolicited. It is that it pushes you to act before you can verify. If the sender wants you to click a link, move the conversation to another app, open an attachment, share a code, or “confirm” something quickly, slow down. Social engineering succeeds by narrowing attention and making the next step feel smaller than it really is [185].

Pay close attention to the sender’s identity, not just the words in the message. A familiar name can be misleading if the account has been copied, compromised, or recently created. Look for small inconsistencies: a username with an extra character, a display name that matches but a handle that does not, a profile photo that seems generic or stolen, or a history that does not fit the claimed role. Be especially cautious when the tone is slightly off. A supposed colleague who suddenly sounds formal, a brand that uses awkward grammar, or a platform account that does not match the service’s usual language may be signaling impersonation. Attackers often rely on the fact that people skim first and verify later.

Comments can be just as useful to an attacker as private messages because they create public pressure. A scam comment may praise your content, warn others about a problem, or direct you to “check your inbox” for a prize, partnership, refund, or security issue. Some comments are designed to bait you into defending yourself publicly so the attacker can keep the exchange going. Others are meant to make your audience click on a link or trust a fake account because it appears underneath a legitimate post. Treat comments that contain urgency, reward language, or requests to leave the platform as suspicious until proven otherwise. If a comment asks you to verify an account, settle a payment, or resolve an issue through an external link, use the platform’s own tools to confirm before responding.

Email remains a favorite channel for phishing because it can be made to look official with very little effort. The red flags are familiar, but they matter more when they are combined: a sender address that is close to a real one but not exact, a generic greeting, a message that creates fear or urgency, and a link that does not match the organization it claims to represent. Fake security notices are especially common. They may say your account will be suspended, your verification has expired, your content violated policy, or your password must be reset immediately. Do not trust the appearance of logos, formatting, or signatures. Those details are easy to copy. What matters is whether the message can be confirmed through the platform itself or through a known official channel you open separately, not by clicking the message's link.

Fake support requests deserve special caution because they exploit trust in help systems. An attacker may pose as platform support, a payment processor, an ad specialist, a copyright agent, or a customer service rep. The request usually sounds procedural: submit a form, confirm your identity, upload a document, approve a login, or share a one-time code so the issue can be resolved. In reality, legitimate support teams do not need your password, MFA code, or recovery code to help you. If someone claiming to be support asks for those things, the request itself is the warning. A real support process should be traceable through the platform's official help center or account dashboard, not through a random message thread.

Another useful habit is to watch for messages that try to move you away from normal verification paths. Scammers often prefer text, private chat, or a third-party form because those spaces are easier to control than the platform's built-in systems. They may ask you to continue on WhatsApp, Telegram, email, or a "secure portal" they provide. They may also insist that the issue is time-sensitive and that using standard support channels will be too slow. That pressure is intentional. If the message asks you to bypass your usual process, treat the bypass itself as suspicious. The safest response is to stop, open the service directly from a saved bookmark or typed address, and verify whether the issue exists at all.

When you are deciding whether a message is legitimate, look for a mismatch between the request and the relationship. A real customer, fan, partner, or platform representative usually has a reason to contact you, but the request should still make sense in context. Does the person know details they should know? Does the tone fit the relationship? Is the request proportionate to the situation, or is it pushing for access, money, or private information too quickly? If the answer feels uncertain, do not let politeness override caution. A short delay is far cheaper than an account recovery process, a stolen identity, or a public breach. Recent work on social engineering and AI-enabled deception shows that attackers are becoming more efficient at tailoring messages and pressure tactics, which makes disciplined verification even more important [33] [186].

Impersonation tactics used against creators, brands, and small businesses

Impersonation aimed at creators, brands, and small businesses usually succeeds because it does not begin with a technical attack. It begins with a believable identity. The attacker copies the visual language of the target, borrows a name that looks close enough to pass quickly, and uses the trust already built around the real account to lower suspicion. In practice, that may mean a fake profile with a nearly identical handle, the same logo, a recycled bio, and a profile image taken from the real page. The goal is not to fool every person forever. The goal is to fool enough people long enough to generate clicks, payments, account access, or reputational damage.

For creators, the impersonator often tries to exploit audience loyalty. A fake account may message followers with a "new partnership," a giveaway, a subscription offer, or a request to move the conversation off-platform. Because audiences are used to seeing direct, informal communication from creators, the scam can feel like a normal extension of the relationship. A similar tactic works against brands: the fake account may pose as customer support, billing, or public relations, then instruct users to "verify" information through a link or a form. Small businesses are especially exposed because customers often expect quick responses and may not distinguish between a real service channel and a convincing duplicate [63]. The attack works best when the impersonator sounds helpful, urgent, and routine at the same time.

One common pattern is the clone account. This is a profile built to look like the original with minimal effort and maximum resemblance. Attackers may copy a recent post, reuse branding assets, and follow the same audience members the real account follows. In some cases, they create slight variations in spelling, punctuation, or added symbols that are easy to miss on a small screen. Another pattern is the hijacked account used as a relay. Instead of creating a fake identity from scratch, the attacker compromises a real follower, partner, or employee account and uses that trusted identity to contact the target. Because the message comes from a known source, the victim is more likely to respond without checking the details.

The risk is not limited to public-facing posts. Impersonation often moves through comments, replies, and direct messages where the social pressure is lower and the interaction feels private. A fake customer may complain publicly to provoke a rushed response. A fake brand partner may send a polished proposal with a request for a media kit, invoice, or "collaboration confirmation." A fake platform representative may claim that the account is at risk unless the user logs in through a special link. These messages are effective because they blend social engineering with brand familiarity. As cybersecurity research continues to show, attackers adapt their methods to the communication habits of the platform rather than relying on one fixed trick [63][33].

Creators and businesses should also watch for impersonation that is less obvious but still damaging. Someone may not copy the account exactly; instead, they may imitate the tone, values, or visual style closely enough to confuse new followers. They may repost content to look legitimate, then use that borrowed credibility to sell unrelated products, solicit donations, or redirect traffic. In more advanced cases, the impersonator uses artificial intelligence to generate messages that sound like the real person or company, making the fake outreach harder to spot at a glance [33][175]. This is one reason a consistent public voice matters: the clearer your real communication style is, the easier it becomes to notice when something feels off.

The best defense starts with making your legitimate presence easier to verify than any imitation. Use the same display name, logo, and biography across platforms where possible, and keep profile links consistent so people can confirm they are in the right place. Claim the obvious variations of your handle before someone else does. Enable verification features where they are available and appropriate, but do not rely on a badge alone; many audiences never look for one. Teach followers and customers where official announcements will appear, what kind of requests you will never send by DM, and how to confirm a message before acting on it. If you run a business, publish a simple support policy that tells people which inboxes are real and which channels you will never use for payment or password recovery.

It also helps to reduce the room impersonators have to improvise. Limit what public information can be used to mimic your operations, such as staff names, internal processes, or exact timing for launches and promotions. Use separate contact addresses for public inquiries, partnerships, and account recovery so a fake request is easier to challenge. Monitor for lookalike accounts, unusual mentions, and sudden spikes in messages from followers asking whether a post or offer is real.

When you find a clone, preserve screenshots, report it through the platform's impersonation tools, and notify your audience through your verified channels. The faster you make the real account visible and the fake account obvious, the less value the impersonation has [191][193].

Urgency, authority, and reward-based manipulation patterns

Urgency is one of the most reliable ways to short-circuit judgment. A message that says your account will be suspended in ten minutes, your payout is on hold, your post violated policy, or your client is waiting for a response is designed to make you move before you verify. On social media, that pressure often arrives in a format that feels normal: a direct message, a comment reply, a brand inquiry, or a support notice that seems to fit the platform. The danger is not only the lie itself; it is the speed it creates. Social engineering works by exploiting human attention, emotion, and decision-making under pressure [195]. If the message is trying to compress your timeline, that compression is the threat.

The safest response to urgency is to slow the interaction down on purpose. Do not click the link, open the attachment, or reply from the message thread just because the wording sounds official. Open the platform separately, navigate to the account or support area yourself, and confirm whether any real issue exists. If the claim concerns payments, policy enforcement, login problems, or account recovery, treat it as unverified until you can confirm it through a trusted channel you initiated. A legitimate platform rarely requires immediate action through a random message thread, and a real business partner can usually tolerate a short verification pause. Any message that punishes caution is asking for trust it has not earned.

Authority-based manipulation uses the same pressure, but with a different emotional lever: deference. Instead of fear, it relies on obedience. The sender may claim to be platform support, a verified brand representative, a manager, a security team member, a lawyer, a vendor, or a high-profile collaborator. The message may include logos, formal language, technical terms, or a polished signature block to imply legitimacy. This is especially effective on social platforms because users are accustomed to fast, informal exchanges and may not pause to question a message that appears to come from someone with status. Impersonation often succeeds by borrowing the visual and social cues of authority before the target has time to inspect the details.

When authority is the hook, verification matters more than tone. A polished message is not proof. A familiar name is not proof. A profile photo, a badge-like symbol, or a convincing email style is not proof. Check the sender identity through an independent route: a known website, a saved contact method, an official help page, or a previously verified business account. If the message claims to come from a colleague, client, or platform representative, confirm it through a separate channel you already trust. This matters because attackers increasingly combine social engineering with automation and generative tools to produce messages that look personalized and credible at scale [5] [33]. The better the imitation, the more important it becomes to verify the source rather than the wording.

Reward-based manipulation is often the most tempting because it offers something instead of threatening something. The lure may be a sponsorship opportunity, a giveaway, a refund, a featured placement, a free product, a collaboration request, a verification badge, or a quick way to recover lost access. The message frames the reward as limited, exclusive, or time-sensitive so that hesitation feels like a missed opportunity. For creators and small businesses, this can be especially effective because the offer seems aligned with real goals: growth, visibility, revenue, or recognition. The attacker is not always asking for money first. Often, they are asking for a login code, a password reset, a payment confirmation, a document, or a move to an outside chat where the pressure can continue without platform oversight.

The right defense is to treat unexpected rewards as suspicious until proven otherwise. Real opportunities can survive a delay for verification. Ask who is offering the reward, how they found you, what the business relationship is, and whether the request can be confirmed through an official domain or a known public contact. If the offer involves prizes, monetization, sponsorship, crypto, or payment processing, be especially careful: these are common themes in fraud because they combine urgency with the promise of gain [130]. If the message asks you to leave the platform, scan a QR code, install software, share a code, or "confirm eligibility" through a strange link, stop there. The reward is being used as a wrapper for access.

The patterns often overlap. A fake support message may begin with urgency, shift into authority, and end with a reward or penalty. A scammer may say your account will be disabled unless you verify it now, but also promise faster monetization or a bonus if you complete the step immediately. That layering is deliberate. It narrows your attention from multiple directions so you have less room to think. The practical defense is not to memorize every possible scam script. It is to recognize the psychological structure underneath the script: pressure, status, and payoff. If a message tries to rush you, outrank you, or entice you into bypassing normal verification, it is operating in the danger zone.

A useful habit is to create a fixed pause before any action that changes access, money, or public trust. That means no immediate clicks on account warnings, no fast responses to high-status requests, and no impulsive acceptance of offers that arrive unexpectedly. Instead, verify the sender, verify the channel, and verify the request. If any part of the message depends on you not checking, that dependence is the warning sign.

Safe verification habits before clicking, paying, or sharing

Before you click a link, send money, or forward a message, slow the process down enough to verify the claim outside the channel where it arrived. That single habit defeats a large share of social media scams because many of them depend on speed, familiarity, and emotional pressure rather than technical sophistication. Social engineering works by pushing you toward an action before you have a chance to compare the request against a trusted source [195][201]. If a message says something is urgent, private, or time-sensitive, treat that urgency as a reason to pause, not a reason to hurry.

Verification should begin with the sender, not the content. Ask whether the account is the one it claims to be, and do not rely on profile photos, display names, or familiar wording alone. Attackers can copy those details easily. Check the handle carefully, review the account history, and look for signs that the profile was created recently, changed names, or has unusually thin activity. If the message appears to come from a friend, coworker, or partner, confirm it through another trusted channel instead of replying inside the same thread. A quick text, phone call, or message to a known number can reveal whether the request is real before you take the next step.

The same rule applies to links, attachments, and payment requests. Do not click simply because a message looks polished or because the sender seems authoritative. Open the platform or company site directly from a saved bookmark or by typing the address yourself, then check whether the claim is visible there. If the message asks you to log in, reset a password, confirm a payout, approve a collaboration, or verify a delivery, treat the request as untrusted until you can reach the destination independently. Many phishing attempts are designed to create a false sense of continuity between the message and the destination, but the safest path is to break that continuity and verify from the outside [198] [202].

For payments, use an especially strict standard. A legitimate business, creator, or vendor should be able to explain exactly what is being charged, who is receiving the money, and why the transaction is necessary. If a request arrives through a direct message or comment thread, confirm the payment details through an official website, known email address, or established client process before sending anything. Be cautious with "refund" schemes, invoice changes, donation requests, emergency fund appeals, and offers that pressure you to move money quickly. If the request involves a new account, a changed bank detail, a gift card, cryptocurrency, or an unfamiliar payment app, stop and verify through another route before proceeding.

Sharing deserves the same discipline as clicking and paying. A message that asks you to repost a warning, forward a giveaway, share a code, or circulate a screenshot may be trying to use your trust to spread the problem further. Before you share, ask whether the information is confirmed, whether the source is original, and whether you are helping the right person or amplifying a fake one. This matters especially when the request involves sensitive personal details, access codes, or "help me recover my account" stories, because attackers often use social proof and emotional urgency to recruit unwitting helpers [201]. If you cannot independently verify the claim, do not help it travel.

A useful rule is to separate recognition from verification. It is fine to notice that a message looks familiar, sounds polite, or uses a logo you recognize. But familiarity is not proof. Verification means checking something that the attacker cannot easily fake at the point of contact.

That might be a known phone number, an official support page, a previously established contact method, or a public announcement from the organization's verified account. When a request concerns your account, your money, or your reputation, the burden of proof should be on the message, not on your instincts.

It also helps to create a personal pause routine for high-risk requests. Read the message once, then step away from it for a moment. Ask four questions: Who is asking? What exactly do they want me to do? Where can I confirm this independently? What happens if I do nothing right now? Those questions slow down the impulse to comply and make it easier to catch manipulation before it works. Research on privacy and security decisions shows that people are often forced into difficult choices under complexity and time pressure, which is exactly why structured nudges and routines improve outcomes [122]. The goal is not to become suspicious of everything. It is to make verification automatic whenever a request involves a click, a payment, or a share that could expose you or others.

CHAPTER 7

Chapter 7: Protecting Content, Brand, and Reputation

Protecting content and reputation requires a different mindset from locking down an account, because the damage here often spreads through reuse, attribution, and perception rather than through direct access alone. A post can be copied, a visual identity can be imitated, and a brand voice can be distorted in ways that are difficult to undo once they circulate. For creators and businesses, that means the work of security extends beyond keeping strangers out; it also includes preserving ownership signals, reducing confusion, and making it easier for an audience to recognize what is genuine.

Copyright, watermarking, and content ownership basics for creators and businesses

Copyright is the legal framework that gives creators and businesses a way to control how original work is copied, shared, adapted, and sold. On social media, that matters because the platform environment is built for speed and reuse. A photo, reel, caption, logo, product shot, or tutorial can be screenshotted, reposted, remixed, or embedded in seconds. Ownership does not disappear just because content becomes easy to circulate, but enforcement becomes harder the longer you wait and the more places the material spreads. For creators, that means your work has value even when it is published publicly. For businesses, it means your marketing assets, product images, and branded language are part of your intellectual property posture, not just your content calendar.

The first habit is to separate ownership from visibility. Posting something publicly may make it available to a wide audience, but it does not automatically transfer the rights to that work to the platform or to other users. At the same time, the terms of service you accept can grant the platform limited rights to host, display, distribute, or process your content in order to operate the service. Those rights are not the same as ownership, and the difference matters when you decide what to post, where to post it, and how much original material to place in a channel that you do not control. If a post is central to your brand, income, or product strategy, treat it as an asset that deserves the same care you would give a file stored in a business archive.

Watermarking is one of the simplest ways to make ownership visible without pretending it is a complete defense. A watermark can help viewers identify the source of an image, video, or graphic at a glance, and it can make casual theft less convenient. It also gives you a public marker that can support attribution when your work travels beyond your profile. But a watermark is not a lock. It can be cropped, blurred, edited, or covered. If you use one, keep it consistent enough to be recognizable but not so intrusive that it ruins the content or encourages you to overstate its protective value. The best watermark is a signal of authorship, not a substitute for documentation.

That documentation is where many creators and small businesses become more secure. Keep original project files, drafts, timestamps, export versions, and publication records in a place you can access later. Save screenshots or links showing when and where the content first appeared. If you work with contractors, photographers, editors, designers, or agencies, make sure the agreement clearly says who owns the final work, what licenses are being granted, and whether the material can be reused in portfolios, ads, or derivative campaigns. A surprising number of disputes are not about whether someone made the content, but about whether the business paid for full ownership or only for limited use. Clear records reduce confusion when a takedown request, licensing question, or impersonation issue appears later.

It is also important to understand how social media changes the practical meaning of "fair use," licensing, and reposting. A platform's repost button, remix feature, or duet tool may make sharing feel routine, but convenience does not erase the need to respect the creator's rights. If you are a business, this matters when your team uses customer photos, influencer clips, or third-party music in promotional content. If you are a creator, it matters when other accounts lift your work and present it as their own. Attribution alone may not be enough, and permission should not be assumed because something is already visible online. When in doubt, use the safest standard: ask before using, credit when authorized, and keep proof of permission in writing.

For businesses, content ownership should be built into the workflow before publication. Decide who can approve final assets, who owns raw files, where those files are stored, and what happens when an employee, freelancer, or agency relationship ends. A social account is easier to protect when the brand also controls its source material, templates, and publishing access. This becomes especially important during a security incident. If a compromised account is used to post false claims, counterfeit offers, or copied material, you need to be able to prove what is authentic, what was authorized, and what was not. That proof is much easier to assemble when your content creation process already includes version control, access limits, and written permissions [209].

Creators should also think about watermarking and ownership as part of reputation management, not only anti-theft strategy. A clear brand mark, a consistent visual style, and a repeatable publishing signature help audiences identify the real source when fake accounts or copied posts appear. Research across digital trust and IP protection continues to show that ownership disputes are increasingly tied to cybersecurity, platform misuse, and rapid content replication rather than to traditional offline copying alone [209]. In other words, protecting content is now inseparable from protecting identity. The more recognizable your work becomes, the more important it is to make the real source easy to verify and the false source easier to challenge.

If you publish highly reusable assets, consider whether different versions deserve different levels of exposure. A final promotional image may be public, while the high-resolution source file, editable template, raw footage, or brand kit should remain private and access-controlled. That separation limits what an outsider can steal if they gain access to one account or one device. It also gives you more leverage if someone copies your work, because you can point to the original file trail, the publication history, and the business records that show who created it and under what terms. In social media security, ownership is not only about legal rights. It is also about being able to prove, preserve, and defend the authenticity of what you publish.

Preventing impersonation and fake account abuse

Impersonation usually works because it does not ask the victim to notice a dramatic lie. It asks them to accept a familiar-looking signal quickly: a name they recognize, a logo they have seen before, a profile photo that seems close enough, or a message written in a voice that feels routine. The attacker's job is to create just enough resemblance to pass the first glance. Your job is to make the first glance less important than the second. That means checking the details that are easy to overlook when you are moving fast: the handle, the spelling, the account age, the follower pattern, the posting history, and whether the profile behaves like a real person or a copy assembled for a single purpose.

For individuals, impersonation may be aimed at stealing attention, extracting money, or embarrassing the real account holder. For creators and businesses, the damage is broader because a fake account can intercept customers, answer questions in the wrong voice, promote counterfeit offers, or claim to be a support channel. The harm is not limited to the fake profile itself. It spreads through confusion. People who cannot immediately tell which account is real may hesitate to engage, and hesitation is expensive when trust is part of the business model [17]. In that sense, impersonation is not only a fraud problem; it is a reputation problem that can reduce reach, weaken credibility, and create support work that never should have existed.

The most effective defense begins with making the authentic account easy to verify. Use a profile name and bio that are consistent across platforms, and keep the public-facing details stable enough that followers can compare them across channels. If the platform offers verification, apply for it when eligible, but do not treat a badge as your only defense. A badge can help, yet it does not replace a clear identity pattern. Make your official website, newsletter, or other primary hub point back to the social accounts you actually control, and do the reverse on the profile itself. When people have a trusted path to confirm who you are, they are less likely to be fooled by a lookalike account.

It also helps to reduce the room for confusion in the first place. Avoid changing your display name, avatar, and bio all at once unless you are doing a coordinated rebrand. Sudden changes make it easier for a fake account to blend into the noise or claim that it is the "new" version of you. Keep a record of your standard branding elements so you can spot copied material quickly. If you run a business or creator account, reserve the same or similar names on major platforms even if you do not actively use all of them. That makes it harder for an imitator to occupy the obvious alternatives and easier for your audience to find the real place to look.

Fake account abuse becomes more dangerous when attackers use scale or automation. AI-generated content can make copied profiles look more polished, more varied, and more believable than older low-effort scams [82]. A fake account no longer needs to rely on broken grammar or obvious stock imagery to appear legitimate. It can borrow real photos, generate plausible captions, and maintain a steady posting rhythm. Research on malicious AI use has warned that these tools can lower the cost of deception and help attackers produce convincing content at speed [5] [61]. That means your verification habits need to focus less on whether a profile looks professional and more on whether it can be independently confirmed.

When you encounter a suspicious account, compare it against the real one instead of judging it in isolation. Check whether the handle differs by a single character, whether the follower count is oddly low or inflated, whether the account has a long gap in activity followed by a burst of posts, and whether the comments look like real engagement or recycled noise. Look at the account's links, tagged posts, and mutual connections. A fake profile often exposes itself through inconsistency: a polished profile image paired with thin history, a business name with no real customer interaction, or a personal account that never behaves like a person. If the account is claiming to be you, your company, or someone you know, compare the content against the known voice, posting style, and network of the genuine profile before responding.

Once you confirm a fake account, act quickly but methodically. Save screenshots, record the profile URL, and note any messages, payment requests, or impersonated brand elements. Then use the platform's reporting tools and, if applicable, notify customers, followers, or partners through your verified channels. If the impersonator is targeting your audience, a brief warning from the real account can prevent a lot of damage. Keep the message simple: identify the official account, state that the other profile is unauthorized, and tell people not to click links, share codes, or send money. The faster you reassert the authentic channel, the less room the fake account has to borrow your trust.

For ongoing protection, make impersonation harder to sustain than it is to launch. Monitor your name, brand, and common misspellings across platforms. Watch for sudden spikes in friend requests, follows, or messages that appear to come from a copied identity. If your audience is large enough, consider publishing a standing note that explains how people can verify official accounts and where they should report suspicious ones. The goal is not to eliminate every fake profile; that is unrealistic. The goal is to make your real identity easy to confirm, your audience harder to mislead, and your response fast enough that a copied name does not become a copied reputation.

Reputation management before, during, and after a security incident

A security incident is never only a technical event. The moment an account is hacked, impersonated, leaked, or used to spread false content, the story becomes public in some form, even if only a few people notice at first. That is why reputation management has to begin before anything goes wrong. Before an incident, the goal is to make your presence easy to recognize as legitimate and hard to confuse with a fake version. Use a consistent name, profile image, bio, and visual style across your main channels so followers can tell what is authentic at a glance. Keep your public contact information current, and make sure customers, collaborators, and followers know the official ways to reach you. If you run a business or public-facing account, consider pinning a post that explains your real support channels and warns people not to trust unsolicited requests for payments, codes, or credential resets.

Pre-incident reputation work also means reducing the amount of confusion an attacker can exploit later. A fake account is more believable when your real account is inconsistent, inactive, or poorly documented. Keep a clear record of your official handles, common display names, and linked sites. If your platform allows it, secure verification badges or other authenticity markers, but do not depend on them alone. Attackers can still imitate the overall look and tone of a trusted profile. Your strongest defense is a recognizable pattern of communication. If you normally post in a certain voice, use the same brand colors, or sign messages in a specific way, that consistency helps your audience spot a mismatch quickly. This matters because reputation attacks often succeed by making people hesitate long enough to click, pay, or share before they verify.

During an incident, speed matters, but so does message discipline. The first public statement should be brief, factual, and calm. Say what happened in plain language, what you know, what you do not yet know, and what people should do next. Avoid speculation, sarcasm, blame, or emotional overexplaining. If the account is compromised, do not use the compromised channel to have a back-and-forth with the attacker or to argue with commenters. Move the audience toward a trusted channel you control, such as a verified website, email list, or alternate social account. If the incident involves impersonation, publish a clear warning that identifies the real account and the fake one, and ask followers not to engage with messages, links, or payment requests coming from the impersonator. In fast-moving online environments, misinformation can spread quickly and cause harm beyond the original breach [17].

A good incident message should also set expectations. People are more forgiving when they understand that you are responding methodically. Let them know whether you are resetting passwords, revoking sessions, contacting platform support, or involving law enforcement if appropriate. If customer data, direct messages, or media files may have been exposed, say that you are investigating the scope rather than pretending certainty you do not have. If you are a creator or small business, designate one person to speak publicly so the message stays consistent across replies, stories, comments, and email. Mixed signals create doubt, and doubt is expensive. A scattered response can make a manageable breach look larger than it is, especially when screenshots and reposts start circulating faster than corrections.

After the immediate threat is contained, reputation work shifts from urgency to trust repair. This is the stage where many people make a mistake by going silent for too long or by posting one vague apology and assuming the matter is closed. Silence leaves room for speculation. Overposting can make the situation look chaotic. The better approach is a measured update that explains what was affected, what has been secured, and what changes are being made to prevent a repeat. If followers or customers were inconvenienced, acknowledge that directly. If there was false content posted from your account, name it as false and correct it clearly. If the incident involved a phishing message sent to your audience, tell people exactly how to identify the scam version and what to do if they already interacted with it. Research on cyber-harm shows that the effects of an attack often spread beyond the immediate technical damage, affecting trust, behavior, and downstream relationships [17].

Reputation recovery is also a documentation task. Save screenshots of fake profiles, malicious posts, support tickets, takedown requests, and public statements. Keep a timeline of what happened and when you responded. That record helps if the issue resurfaces later, if a platform asks for evidence, or if a partner wants confirmation of how the incident was handled. It also helps you review whether your public messaging was clear enough. In many cases, the strongest long-term repair comes from visible competence: you identified the problem quickly, communicated honestly, and tightened the weak points that made the incident possible. If the attack used manipulated media, such as a fake audio clip or altered video, you may need to be especially direct, because synthetic media can make false claims look convincing at first glance [4]. In that situation, the best reputation defense is not outrage; it is clarity, documentation, and repeated confirmation of the authentic source.

Creating a consistent voice and approval process for public posts

A consistent voice is a security control as much as it is a branding choice. When followers, customers, and partners can reliably recognize how you speak, what you promise, and how you handle problems, it becomes harder for an impostor to sound convincing. A fake account can copy a logo or reuse a photo, but it is much harder to fake a stable pattern of wording, tone, and decision-making over time. That matters because impersonation often succeeds in the first few seconds, before anyone has time to investigate closely. The more predictable and disciplined your public voice is, the easier it is for others to spot when something feels off.

Consistency does not mean sounding robotic. It means defining the boundaries of your public identity so your posts do not drift with every mood, trend, or platform. Decide what your account is known for: the subjects you speak about, the level of formality you use, the words you avoid, and the kind of claims you never make casually. If you run a business or creator account, document the basics in a simple style guide. Include preferred names, pronouns if relevant, brand terms, hashtags, emoji use, punctuation habits, and the tone you use when responding to praise, complaints, or urgent issues. This kind of structure reduces accidental disclosure and keeps your public profile from becoming easier to imitate through inconsistency.

A defined voice also helps protect you during stress. When a scam, controversy, or security incident appears, people often write too quickly and say more than they intended. That is when a style guide becomes useful. It gives you a standard to return to when emotions are high and time is short. A calm, familiar tone can prevent a response from sounding panicked, defensive, or fragmented. It also makes it easier for your audience to tell the difference between an official statement and a hurried imitation. In that sense, voice is part of reputation defense: it helps preserve trust when the situation is unstable.

Approval processes matter most when more than one person can publish on behalf of an account. The risk is not only that someone will post the wrong thing; it is that a well-meaning person will post something accurate but poorly timed, poorly worded, or too revealing. A simple review process creates a pause between drafting and publishing, which is often enough to catch mistakes before they become public. For a solo creator, that process may be as basic as rereading a post after stepping away for a few minutes and checking it against a short checklist. For a small business, it may involve one person drafting and another approving anything that mentions pricing, legal claims, partnerships, customer issues, or security-sensitive information.

The approval process should match the risk level of the content. Not every post needs formal review, but some posts should never go out casually. Anything involving financial offers, account recovery, customer data, urgent announcements, giveaways, policy disputes, or changes to contact information deserves extra scrutiny. So do posts that include screenshots, internal conversations, location details, staff names, unpublished products, or references to current incidents. If your team uses scheduling tools, build approval into the workflow before the post is queued. A post that has already been scheduled can still be edited or canceled, but it is far easier to catch problems before publication than after the audience has seen them.

The best approval process is one people can actually follow. If it is too slow, too complex, or too dependent on memory, it will be skipped when deadlines get tight. Keep it simple: draft, verify, approve, publish. Define who can approve what, how urgent posts are handled, and what happens when the normal approver is unavailable. Make sure the reviewer is checking for more than grammar. They should look for accuracy, tone, privacy exposure, brand consistency, and whether the post could be misread if taken out of context. This kind of review reflects a broader security principle: reducing preventable mistakes by adding a small amount of friction before action [151].

It also helps to separate content creation from final authority. The person who writes a post should not always be the person who decides it is ready, especially if the post affects customers, partners, or the public image of the account. In a small team, that separation may be informal, but it should still be real. Even one extra set of eyes can catch a typo in a link, a misleading phrase, an accidental disclosure, or a screenshot that reveals more than intended. If you are working alone, create your own approval ritual. Read the post aloud, check every name and link, and ask whether the wording would still be appropriate if it were screenshotted and shared without context.

Keep records of your standards, not just your posts. A short archive of approved phrasing for common situations can save time and reduce inconsistency. Examples include responses to customer complaints, partnership inquiries, technical issues, and security notices. These templates should be adaptable, not copied blindly, but they give you a safe starting point when you need to respond quickly. Over time, that combination of voice discipline and approval structure makes your public presence more resilient. It reduces the chance that a rushed post will create confusion, weaken trust, or give an attacker an easy opening to exploit.

CHAPTER 8

Chapter 8: Securing Devices, Networks, and Connected Tools

The devices and tools that support a social media presence are often treated as background infrastructure, yet they are part of the same exposure surface as the account itself. A phone, laptop, tablet, browser, or connected app can quietly shape what gets seen, what gets saved, and what can be reached if something goes wrong. That is why security here is less about adding one more layer of caution and more about making the environment itself harder to misuse. In practice, the goal is to reduce avoidable weakness before it can be combined with a password leak, a phishing message, or a compromised session.

Device hygiene: updates, screen locks, encryption, and app permissions

A secure social media account depends on the device it runs on. If the phone, tablet, or laptop is easy to unlock, poorly maintained, or overexposed to unnecessary apps, the account inherits those weaknesses no matter how strong the password may be. That is why device hygiene is not a separate technical chore; it is part of account protection. The goal is to make the device harder to tamper with, harder to read, and harder to use as a bridge into your social presence.

Updates are the first layer of that hygiene. Operating system patches, browser updates, and app updates often close flaws that attackers can exploit without any dramatic warning. Delaying them leaves known weaknesses in place, and those weaknesses are especially risky on devices used for messaging, posting, and account recovery. The practical habit is simple: enable automatic updates where possible and treat update prompts as maintenance, not interruptions. This matters for more than convenience. In socio-technical environments, small lapses in upkeep often become the point where broader risk starts to spread [218]. A device that is current is not immune, but it is far less likely to be undermined by a vulnerability that has already been fixed.

Screen locks are equally basic and equally important. If someone can pick up your phone and open it without resistance, they may not need to hack anything. They may be able to read direct messages, approve login prompts, reset passwords through stored email access, or post before you notice. Use a lock method that fits the device and your daily routine, but do not settle for the weakest option simply because it is fast. A short PIN is better than no lock, but a longer passcode, biometric unlock paired with a strong backup code, or a similar higher-friction method provides better protection. The point is not to make the device annoying to use. It is to make casual access difficult enough that a lost, borrowed, or unattended device does not become an open door.

Encryption adds another layer by protecting the data stored on the device itself. Many modern phones and laptops encrypt storage by default, but that protection is only useful if you keep the device locked and the software updated. Encryption is what helps keep local data from being immediately readable if the hardware is lost or stolen. For social media users, that local data may include saved passwords, authentication tokens, private photos, drafts, message previews, and cached account information. In other words, the device may hold more than you realize, even when the app looks empty. Human-centered security research consistently shows that people's everyday practices and device settings strongly shape real-world exposure, especially when private information is stored or accessed through connected tools [219]. If you are not sure whether encryption is enabled, check the security settings of the operating system rather than assuming it is active.

App permissions deserve the same attention because they determine what an app can reach once installed. A social media app may reasonably need access to your camera, microphone, photos, or notifications, but that does not mean every permission should stay on by default forever. A scheduling tool may not need your contacts. A photo editor may not need location access. A quiz app or trend filter may ask for more than it truly requires. Review permissions periodically and remove anything that is not clearly tied to the app's purpose. This is especially important because many privacy harms do not come from one malicious app; they come from a collection of ordinary apps that each collect a little too much. The more tools you allow onto the device, the more careful you have to be about what each one can see, store, and share.

It also helps to think in terms of separation. The same device can be used safely for personal and professional social media work, but only if you avoid unnecessary overlap. Do not install every experimental app on the phone you use for account recovery. Do not grant business tools access to personal photo libraries unless there is a clear reason. Do not let consumer apps sit alongside creator or admin tools without reviewing what they can reach. This is less about paranoia than about reducing the number of places where one mistake can cascade. If a device is shared with family members, assistants, or team members, the need for clean boundaries becomes even more important. The more people who can touch the device, the more disciplined the lock screen, update routine, and permission review need to be.

A practical review does not have to be complicated. Check whether automatic updates are on. Confirm that the screen lock cannot be bypassed with a simple gesture or a weak code. Verify that storage encryption is enabled if the device supports it. Then inspect app permissions one by one and remove anything unnecessary. If a platform or connected tool asks for a permission that seems unrelated to its function, pause before approving it. That pause is often what keeps a convenience feature from becoming a security problem. On a social media device, hygiene is not about making the system perfect. It is about making the most common mistakes harder to make and the most damaging mistakes easier to catch early.

Safe use of public Wi-Fi, mobile hotspots, and shared devices

Public Wi-Fi is convenient because it removes friction, but that same convenience removes a layer of trust. In a café, airport, hotel, library, or conference center, you usually do not control who else is on the network, how the network is configured, or whether the connection name is even legitimate. An attacker does not need to break into your account first if they can sit between your device and the service you are trying to reach. That is why public networks should be treated as untrusted by default, even when they require a password or appear to be offered by a reputable business.

The safest habit is to assume that anything sensitive should wait until you are on a network you control. If you can avoid it, do not log in to social accounts on public Wi-Fi to change passwords, review recovery settings, approve login prompts, or handle direct messages that involve money, contracts, or personal data. If you must use public Wi-Fi, keep the session narrow. Open only the app or site you need, complete the task, and sign out when finished. Avoid saving passwords in shared browsers, avoid checking “remember me” on unfamiliar devices, and avoid using automatic connection features that can silently reconnect you to a network you did not mean to trust.

A mobile hotspot is usually a better choice than public Wi-Fi because it places the connection under your control. Even so, a hotspot is not automatically safe just because it is private. The phone or hotspot device still needs a strong passcode, current software, and a name that does not reveal too much about you. If you use your phone as a hotspot for social media work, keep the device locked, disable hotspot sharing when you are done, and avoid leaving it open in crowded places where strangers can guess that you are offering a connection. If the hotspot is for business use, do not let it become a casual default for every device and every task. A controlled connection is useful precisely because it is controlled.

Some of the most overlooked risks come from shared devices. A hotel business center computer, a coworking station, a borrowed tablet, a school lab machine, or a family member's laptop may seem harmless for a quick check-in, but shared systems are built for convenience, not privacy. Browsers may retain history, cookies, autofill data, and session tokens after you close the window. Keyboard shortcuts, clipboard contents, and cached logins can also expose information to the next person who uses the device. If you absolutely must use a shared device, use private browsing only as a small safeguard, not a full solution. Sign in only to the minimum needed account, avoid downloading files, do not upload recovery codes or sensitive images, and make sure you fully sign out before walking away.

It is also worth paying attention to the network names and login pages themselves. Public environments are vulnerable to lookalike hotspots that copy the name of a real venue in order to lure people into connecting. A network called "Hotel_Guest" or "Airport_Free_WiFi" may be legitimate, or it may be an imitation created to capture traffic.

Verify the exact network name with staff rather than guessing. If a browser login page asks for unusual permissions, downloads a certificate, or requests more information than a normal guest portal should need, stop and reassess. Social media access is rarely worth forcing through a suspicious network prompt.

For creators and small businesses, the risk is not just account access; it is also workflow exposure. A quick post drafted on a shared laptop may leave behind drafts, captions, brand assets, analytics screenshots, customer names, or payment details. A mobile hotspot used during travel may be the better option, but it should still be paired with device hygiene: screen lock, automatic updates, remote wipe capability, and a browser that does not sync sensitive work to a shared profile. Research on connected systems consistently shows that as more devices and services become linked, the attack surface expands with them [63]. The same principle applies here: every extra device, network, or login path is another place where control can slip.

A simple rule helps keep these situations manageable: public means temporary, hotspot means controlled, and shared means exposed. If you remember that distinction, you are less likely to treat convenience as safety. Use the least trusted environment only for the least sensitive task, and move anything important back to a device and connection you can actually govern.

Risks from scheduling tools, analytics apps, and browser extensions

Scheduling tools, analytics apps, and browser extensions are attractive because they make social media easier to manage, but they also sit very close to the center of your account activity. They often need broad permissions to post on your behalf, read performance data, access messages, or interact with the browser session where you are already signed in. That convenience creates a practical security tradeoff: the more a tool can do for you, the more damage it can cause if it is compromised, poorly designed, or simply no longer trustworthy. In a connected environment where many services exchange data continuously, one weak link can expose far more than the tool's own dashboard suggests [63][233].

Scheduling platforms deserve special caution because they are built to act with your authority. If you connect one to a business profile, creator account, or shared team workspace, it may gain the ability to publish content, delete drafts, approve comments, or route messages without requiring a fresh login each time. That means a stolen token or compromised vendor account can become a publishing channel for spam, scams, or misinformation. Even when the tool itself is legitimate, a misconfigured integration can expose content calendars, draft campaigns, internal notes, or customer responses to people who should never see them. For a public-facing account, that is not just an operational problem; it is a trust problem.

Analytics apps create a different kind of exposure. They usually promise insight into audience growth, engagement, best times to post, or competitor tracking, and many of them collect enough account data to build detailed behavioral profiles. Those profiles can reveal patterns about when you are online, what content performs best, which posts you are preparing, and how your audience responds to certain themes. That information may seem harmless in isolation, but it becomes useful to attackers when combined with public posts, follower relationships, and visible routines. In some cases, the app is less dangerous because it is malicious and more dangerous because it is over-privileged. It asks for access that exceeds what it truly needs, and users accept the request because the feature looks useful.

Browser extensions deserve the same level of scrutiny, if not more. Extensions can read and modify what you see in the browser, capture form data, inject content into pages, and interact with sessions that are already authenticated. That makes them powerful productivity tools, but also a common source of hidden risk. A seemingly harmless extension for grammar checking, image downloading, link shortening, or social media enhancement may have access to every tab you open, including login pages, direct messages, and admin dashboards. If the extension is sold, updated into something more aggressive, or silently abused by an attacker, it can become a surveillance layer inside the browser itself. Because extensions often feel like part of the browser rather than outside software, people forget they are granting ongoing access to a highly sensitive workspace.

The safest way to evaluate these tools is to treat them like vendors, not accessories. Ask what data they collect, what permissions they request, how they authenticate, whether they support least-privilege access, and how they handle account deletion or token revocation. If a scheduling app wants access to multiple social profiles when you only need one, that is a warning sign. If an analytics service requires broad message access to produce basic engagement reports, that is another. If a browser extension has not been updated in a long time, has unclear ownership, or is installed simply because it was recommended in a tutorial, it should be reviewed or removed. Security often fails not because the user ignored a major red flag, but because they accepted a small one without examining the pattern.

It also helps to separate convenience from core access. A tool that makes posting faster should not be the same tool that controls your password recovery, your primary email, or your business payment flow. Keep the number of connected services as small as possible, and prefer tools that can operate with limited permissions rather than full account control. Review connected apps regularly from the platform's security settings, not from the app's own dashboard alone. If you stop using a service, revoke its access completely instead of assuming inactivity makes it harmless. Tokens, cached sessions, and third-party permissions can remain valid long after you have forgotten the app exists.

For teams, the risk increases when tools are shared informally. One employee may install an extension to save time, another may connect a scheduler to a personal profile, and a third may use an analytics app without documenting what it can reach. That kind of shadow access is hard to audit later, especially if staff turn over or contractors come and go. A cleaner workflow is to assign one person to approve connected tools, keep a simple inventory of what each service can access, and remove anything that no longer has a clear business purpose. On social media, the most dangerous tools are not always the obvious scams. Often they are the legitimate services that were given too much trust for too long.

Separating personal, creator, and business workflows where possible

When possible, keep personal, creator, and business activity in separate lanes instead of letting one account, one device, or one login session do every job. The reason is simple: once workflows overlap, the weakest part of the setup can expose everything else. A personal profile may need relaxed social interaction, a creator account may need public engagement and publishing tools, and a business account may need shared access, customer support, and administrative oversight. Those needs are not the same, and treating them as if they are invites avoidable risk. Access control works best when permissions are limited to what each role actually needs [236].

The cleanest separation begins with the accounts themselves. If you manage your own presence, your creator brand, and a business page, avoid signing all three into the same browser profile or the same device user account unless there is no realistic alternative. Separate browser profiles, separate password vault entries, and separate recovery emails reduce the chance that one compromise turns into a full chain reaction. If a personal device is also used for business publishing, the attack surface grows with every extra app, extension, and saved login. The goal is not perfection; it is to make cross-contamination harder. A personal mistake should not automatically grant access to a customer list, a brand page, or a monetized channel.

In practice, that means deciding which tools belong to which lane. Your personal workflow should stay as close as possible to ordinary use: direct messaging, private sharing, and limited connected services. A creator workflow should be built around content production, scheduling, analytics, and audience interaction, but with minimal access to private family or personal correspondence. A business workflow should be even more deliberate, because it often includes shared credentials, ad accounts, payment systems, and support inboxes. If a tool is only needed for one lane, do not let it follow you into the others. Third-party applications often request broad permissions, and those permissions should be reviewed in the context of the role they serve rather than accepted as a convenience tax [236].

This separation also applies to content handling. Personal photos, drafts, campaign assets, invoices, screenshots, and customer messages should not all live in the same camera roll or downloads folder if you can avoid it. Use distinct cloud folders, naming conventions, and storage locations so that accidental sharing becomes less likely. A post intended for a business audience should not be one tap away from a private album. Likewise, creator assets should not be mixed with personal documents that reveal addresses, travel plans, or family details. The more clearly your files are organized, the easier it is to spot what should never be published, forwarded, or attached to a message.

If you work with assistants, partners, or staff, role separation becomes even more important. Shared access should be granted through the smallest practical permission set, not through a single master login that everyone uses because it is faster. One person may need to schedule posts, another may need to respond to comments, and another may need to manage ads or billing. Those are different functions, and they should not be bundled unless the platform offers no better option. Modern security guidance consistently emphasizes limiting access to the minimum necessary scope so that one compromised credential does not expose unrelated resources [236]. If your platform allows role-based access, use it. If it does not, compensate by reducing who can sign in, where they can sign in from, and what they can change.

Device separation is equally valuable. If your personal phone is used for creator work late at night and business work in the morning, the same notifications, autofill data, and app permissions can bleed across all three contexts. A simpler model is to designate one device or browser profile for high-trust personal use and another for public-facing or administrative work. Even if you cannot maintain fully separate hardware, you can still separate the environment: different email accounts, different saved sessions, different authentication apps, and different folders for downloads and media. That structure helps during incidents too. If one workflow is compromised, you can isolate it more quickly because you already know which tools and credentials belong to it.

The same discipline should guide everyday habits. Do not forward business messages into personal chats just because it is convenient. Do not use a creator account to test random apps that you would never permit on a business profile. Do not store recovery codes in the same note, document, or screenshot folder as personal reminders. Small shortcuts are how workflows become entangled, and entangled workflows are how a routine login problem becomes a broader security event. Separation does not slow you down as much as it seems; once it becomes habitual, it actually reduces confusion. You spend less time wondering which account to use, which device is safe, and which permission belongs to which role. That clarity is a security control in its own right.

CHAPTER 9

Chapter 9: Incident Response for Social Media Breaches

When a social media account is breached, speed matters, but so does order. The first minutes are rarely the time for perfect answers; they are the time for controlled action, clear observation, and disciplined communication. A breach can involve more than a stolen password: it may include unauthorized posts, changed recovery details, hijacked messages, copied content, or an impostor using your name to reach other people. Because the damage can spread through trust as quickly as through access, your response has to be organized around both containment and credibility. That means knowing what to secure first, what to preserve, and what to say before confusion fills the gap.

Immediate steps to contain damage and regain control

When you discover that an account has been compromised, the first objective is not to fix everything at once. It is to stop the damage from spreading. That means acting on the most urgent threats first: unauthorized access, unauthorized posting, altered recovery details, and any connected services that could be used to reach other accounts. If you hesitate while trying to understand every detail, the attacker keeps control of the environment and may continue using your profile as a trusted channel to reach followers, customers, or contacts. Treat the situation as active containment, not as a routine troubleshooting task.

Start by removing the attacker's easiest path back in. If you can still sign in, change the password immediately from a device you trust and make the new password unique. If the platform offers a "log out of all sessions" or "sign out of other devices" option, use it after the password change so any existing sessions are invalidated. Review the account's recovery email address, phone number, and linked authentication methods next. Attackers often try to replace these quietly, because recovery settings can be more valuable than the password itself. If anything has been changed, restore it to your own contact information right away and remove unfamiliar recovery methods before moving on.

Then inspect the account for signs of misuse that are easy to miss in the first rush. Look at recent posts, stories, messages, comments, and profile edits. Delete or hide anything you did not create, especially if it contains links, promises, requests for money, or messages that could embarrass you or mislead others. Check direct messages for outgoing spam, fraudulent offers, or replies sent in your name. Review your bio, display name, profile photo, website link, and any pinned content, because those are often changed to support impersonation or redirect traffic. If the platform provides an activity log, use it to identify suspicious logins, new devices, or unfamiliar locations. If there are connected apps or third-party tools you do not recognize, revoke their access immediately.

Containment should extend beyond the social platform itself. If the same password, recovery email, or phone number is used elsewhere, assume the compromise may have broader reach. Secure the recovery email account first, because it is often the key to resetting other services. If your social account is tied to payment tools, scheduling software, ad accounts, or cloud storage, review those connections for unusual activity and remove any unfamiliar permissions. On a business account, check whether the breach could affect customer support channels, storefront links, or team access. The point is to cut off every bridge the attacker could use to move from one service to another [247].

If you cannot regain access quickly, switch from containment inside the account to containment around it. Warn your audience through a separate trusted channel that the account is compromised and that any unusual messages, links, or requests should be ignored. Keep the notice short and factual. Do not speculate about the cause or argue with the attacker publicly. If the platform allows you to report the takeover, do so through the official recovery or abuse process as soon as possible. For creators and small businesses, it may also be necessary to notify partners, team members, or customers who could be targeted through the fake account. A clear warning can prevent the incident from becoming a larger trust problem.

Preserve evidence while you work, but do not let documentation delay urgent action. Save screenshots of suspicious posts, messages, login alerts, profile changes, and any email notices related to the breach. Record timestamps, device names, and anything else that may help explain the sequence of events later. This is useful not only for platform reporting, but also for understanding how the attacker got in and whether the compromise involved phishing, reused credentials, or a weak recovery path. Digital evidence can be fragile, and once content is deleted or edited, reconstructing the timeline becomes harder [244].

As soon as the immediate threat is under control, check the rest of your security setup for weaknesses that may have allowed the incident. If you reused the compromised password anywhere else, change those passwords too. If the breach involved a phone number, email account, or authentication app, secure those channels before returning to normal use. If the account belongs to a team or family member, make sure everyone who has access understands what happened and what to look for next. The goal is not only to regain control of one profile, but to prevent the same weakness from reopening the door. In a social media incident, speed matters, but disciplined order matters more: stop the spread, remove the attacker's access, verify the account, and then rebuild from a stable position.

How to document evidence and report abuse effectively

The quality of your response to an abuse incident often depends on what you can prove, not just what you can describe. Platforms, payment providers, and law enforcement all work faster when you can show a clear sequence: what happened, when it happened, where it appeared, and how it affected the account or audience. Start by preserving the original evidence before you begin deleting posts, changing settings, or contacting support. Take screenshots that include the full screen, the username or handle, the date and time if visible, and any URL or platform context. If the problem involves a message thread, capture the entire conversation, not only the threatening or suspicious line. If the abuse is in a story, reel, live stream, or disappearing message, record the screen as soon as possible, because those items can vanish quickly.

A useful evidence file is organized around events, not feelings. Create a simple incident log and write down each action as it occurs: when you noticed the issue, what account or device you were using, what you saw, what you clicked, what changed, and what you did next. Keep the wording factual. "At 8:14 p.m., I received a direct message from @example_support asking me to verify my account through a link" is more useful than "Someone tried to scam me." If an account was impersonating you, note the exact handle, profile image, bio text, follower count, and any posts or messages that show the impersonation.

If the abuse includes financial loss, write down amounts, transaction IDs, and the payment method used. If there are witnesses, ask them to save their own screenshots and note what they observed independently.

When possible, preserve evidence in more than one format. Screenshots are useful for quick reporting, but they can be questioned if they do not show enough context. Save the page source or copy the profile URL, message link, post link, or support ticket number if the platform provides one. If the platform allows downloads of your data, request them early, before the account is altered further. For video or audio abuse, keep the original file intact and avoid editing it into shorter clips for convenience; make a separate copy for sharing and keep the original unchanged. If the incident involves a browser page, note the browser name, device, operating system, and whether you were signed in. Those details can help support teams understand whether the issue is tied to a particular session or device.

Do not let the process of collecting evidence put you at greater risk. If an attacker still has access, avoid engaging in long exchanges, clicking unknown links, or logging into the account from an untrusted device just to "check one more thing." Use a secure device, and if possible, a separate cloud folder or local drive for the evidence archive. Name files consistently so they are easy to sort later, such as date, platform, account name, and event type. A folder structure like "2026-05-20_Instagram_impersonation" is far easier to use under pressure than a string of random screenshots. If your case may become a legal matter, keep the original files untouched and make copies for reporting. The original version is your strongest record of what was actually seen.

Reporting works best when you match the report to the right channel and keep the message short, direct, and specific. Use the platform's abuse, impersonation, harassment, phishing, or account recovery forms rather than sending a vague complaint through a general inbox. In the report, identify the exact account or content, explain why it violates policy, and include the most important proof first. If the platform asks for links, provide them. If it asks for dates, include them. If it asks for a statement of harm, keep it concrete: "This account is using my name and photo to message my followers" is stronger than a long emotional explanation that buries the key facts. If the issue involves a fake brand page, include the legitimate account name and any public page that shows the real identity, so the reviewer can compare them quickly.

When abuse crosses platforms, repeat the same core facts without rewriting the story each time. The details should stay consistent across support tickets, bank disputes, platform reports, and any police or legal filing. Inconsistent dates, handles, or screenshots can slow the response or weaken the case. If you are reporting phishing or impersonation, notify any affected partner, customer, or collaborator directly if they may be targeted next. If the incident involves a deepfake or manipulated media, note exactly what is fabricated and where it was posted; harmful synthetic content can move quickly and is harder to correct once it spreads [4][5][123]. Keep your communication calm and factual. The goal is to make it easy for the reviewer to verify the abuse and act on it, not to persuade them with volume.

Finally, treat every report as a record you may need again later. Save copies of submitted forms, ticket numbers, chat transcripts, email replies, and any automated acknowledgments. If the platform removes the content or disables the account, keep the confirmation message. If nothing happens after the first report, follow up with the same evidence rather than starting from scratch. A clean paper trail matters because social media incidents often involve overlapping problems: a fake profile, a stolen identity, a compromised inbox, and a misleading message all at once. The more clearly you document each piece, the easier it becomes to separate what the platform should remove, what a service provider should reverse, and what may require a broader legal or security response.

Communicating with followers, customers, and partners during an incident

When an incident is active, your communication should do three things at once: reduce confusion, preserve credibility, and keep people from being harmed by rumors or impersonation. That is harder than it sounds, because the first instinct in a breach is often either silence or overexplanation. Silence can make followers and customers assume the worst, while too much detail can give an attacker useful information, expose unfinished facts, or create contradictions that are hard to correct later. The goal is not to narrate every technical step in real time. It is to give the right people enough information to stay safe, understand what is happening, and know where to look for verified updates.

Start by deciding who needs to hear from you first. A private account with a small network may only require a direct message to close contacts and a public note to anyone who might be affected. A creator, small business, or partner-facing brand usually needs a broader sequence: internal team members, customer-facing channels, business partners, and then the public audience. This order matters because the people closest to the account often become your first line of support, and they also need to know not to trust future messages that look unusual. If a scammer is already using your name, your own communication must help others distinguish your legitimate updates from the fake ones. Consistent wording, a recognizable sender, and a single official channel for updates reduce the chance that people will follow the wrong instructions.

Your first message should be short, factual, and action-oriented. Say what is known, what is not yet known, and what people should do right now. If an account has been compromised, tell followers not to click links, send money, share codes, or respond to unusual requests from that account until you confirm control. If customer data or payment tools may be involved, direct people to monitor their accounts and verify any unexpected emails or messages through a known contact method. Avoid speculation about how the incident happened unless you are certain. A calm, plain statement is more trustworthy than a dramatic explanation that later changes. Research on misinformation and manipulation shows that confusion spreads quickly when people receive incomplete or conflicting signals, especially in fast-moving online environments [72].

For businesses and creators, it helps to separate operational updates from reputation management. Operational updates answer the practical question: what should people do now? Reputation messages answer the social question: can people still trust this account, this offer, or this relationship? Both matter, but they should not be mixed into a single rushed post. If a partner, sponsor, or customer is waiting on a response, send a direct, verified notice through a known channel and repeat the same core facts publicly if needed. If the incident affects scheduled content, payments, shipping, or support response times, name those impacts clearly. People are usually more forgiving of a disruption than of uncertainty, and they are less likely to panic when they can see that you are organized and responsive.

Be especially careful about where you publish updates. If the compromised account is still under attacker control, do not rely on that same account as your only source of truth. Post from a separate verified channel if you have one, such as a backup account, website notice, email list, or business page that is not affected. Then point everyone to that channel for continuing updates. This matters because attackers often use the confusion around an incident to intensify the damage: they may send fake recovery instructions, ask followers to "confirm" information, or imitate your apology style to keep the deception going. A stable communication pattern makes impersonation harder. Use the same official link, the same support email, and the same naming convention every time you update people.

Do not let urgency push you into promising more than you can deliver. It is better to say, "We are investigating and will update by 3:00 p.m. Eastern," than to guess at a cause or timeline. If you miss a promised update time, send a brief correction instead of disappearing. That small act preserves trust more effectively than a polished statement that arrives too late. When you do have new facts, correct the earlier message plainly. Do not bury the correction in a long thread or assume people will notice a quiet edit. In an incident, clarity is a security control. The more readable your communication is, the less room there is for rumors, fake screenshots, and opportunistic copycats to shape the story for you.

It also helps to prepare language for the most common scenarios before you need it. A short incident template can include a notice of unauthorized activity, a warning about suspicious messages, a pointer to the official update channel, and a reminder that you will never ask for passwords, recovery codes, or payment details through direct message. That last point is important because attackers often exploit the moment after an incident by posing as support, recovery agents, or collaborators. If your audience already knows your verification rule, they are less likely to fall for a second scam while you are still recovering from the first. In practice, good incident communication is not only about speaking to the crowd. It is about reducing the number of ways the crowd can be used against you.

Recovery, post-incident review, and rebuilding trust

After the immediate crisis is contained, the next task is to make sure the incident is understood well enough that it does not repeat. That begins with a careful review of what actually happened, not just what was visible on the surface. A post-incident review should trace the sequence from the first warning sign to the final corrective action: how the breach was discovered, which account or device was first affected, what the attacker changed, how long the exposure lasted, and which responses worked quickly versus which ones slowed recovery. This is the point where you move from reaction to analysis. The goal is not to assign blame to yourself, a teammate, or a platform. The goal is to identify the path the attacker took and the conditions that made that path possible.

One useful way to structure the review is to separate the incident into access, impact, and response. Access asks how the attacker got in or got enough leverage to act. Impact asks what they could see, change, publish, send, or copy while inside. Response asks what you did, in what order, and how effective each action was. That distinction matters because the same event can have different root causes: a stolen password, a compromised email account, a reused session on a shared device, a malicious connected app, or a successful impersonation that tricked someone else into granting access. If you only look at the final symptom, you may miss the real weak point. Security research across digital systems consistently shows that incidents often involve layered exposures rather than a single failure [140][252].

Document the facts while they are still fresh. Write down the timeline, the names of the affected accounts, the devices involved, the recovery methods that were changed, and the exact content that was posted or sent without authorization. Keep screenshots, login alerts, support tickets, message threads, and any email notifications related to the event. If a customer, follower, or partner was misled, note how they were contacted and what the attacker tried to accomplish. This record is useful for support teams, but it is also useful for your own review because memory tends to smooth over the sequence of events. The more precise your notes, the easier it becomes to see whether the incident started with a phishing message, a weak recovery channel, a third-party tool, or a device that had not been secured properly.

Once the facts are organized, review the controls that failed to stop the incident and the ones that limited damage. Maybe multi-factor authentication was enabled, but the attacker still got in through a trusted email account. Maybe the password was strong, but a connected scheduling app had broader access than expected. Maybe the account itself was recovered quickly, but the impersonation content stayed visible long enough to confuse followers. These details matter because they show where to strengthen the system. A good review asks not only, "What went wrong?" but also, "What was still effective, and how can we build on that?" In a fast-moving digital environment, resilience comes from reducing the number of paths an attacker can use, not from assuming one control will solve everything [56][252].

The review should also include the human side of the incident. Many people know, in theory, that they should verify requests and react slowly to urgency, but in practice they still click, reply, or approve because the message feels plausible in the moment. That is not a reason for shame; it is a reason to adjust the process. If the incident involved a rushed decision, a missed alert, or a delayed report, identify the conditions that made the mistake more likely. Was the warning buried among routine notifications? Was the recovery process too confusing? Did you rely on memory instead of a written procedure? Behavioral studies of breach response show that people do not always react immediately or consistently after an incident, which makes clear routines and simple follow-up steps especially important [257]. The point is to design around ordinary attention limits, not pretend they do not exist.

Rebuilding trust starts with visible consistency. If the account was used to send false messages, post misleading content, or imitate your voice, followers and customers will judge recovery partly by how stable and recognizable your response becomes afterward. That means restoring the account cleanly, confirming what changed, and then returning to a normal tone and posting pattern once the situation is secure. If you need to explain the incident publicly, keep the message factual and limited to what people need to know: what happened, what they should ignore, what actions you have taken, and how they can confirm future communication is legitimate. Overexplaining can create confusion, while silence can leave room for rumors or continued impersonation. Trust is rebuilt through repeated proof that the account is controlled, the message is authentic, and the safeguards are stronger than before.

For businesses and creators, trust may also need to be rebuilt outside the platform. Partners may want reassurance about payment details, customer support channels, or approval procedures. Followers may need a reminder about the official handle, the correct website, or the types of messages you will never send. If the incident exposed a broader weakness, such as shared access without clear ownership or a lack of review before publishing, put that change in writing and apply it consistently. A post-incident review is only useful if it produces a revised operating pattern. The purpose is not to dwell on what was lost; it is to make the next incident harder to execute, easier to detect, and less damaging if it still occurs.

CHAPTER 10

Chapter 10: Creating a Sustainable Safety Routine

A sustainable safety routine is what turns good intentions into something you can actually maintain when work gets busy, attention drifts, or the platform changes under you. The point is not to live in a constant state of vigilance; it is to build a rhythm that keeps basic protections from slipping while still leaving room for normal use. That rhythm needs to be light enough to repeat, clear enough to follow without hesitation, and flexible enough to fit different roles without becoming a burden. In practice, the strongest routines are the ones that reduce decision fatigue and make security feel like part of ordinary account care rather than a special project.

Weekly, monthly, and quarterly social media security routines

A sustainable routine works best when it is divided by cadence, not by mood. Weekly checks handle the fast-moving risks: unauthorized logins, unexpected messages, new follower requests, and changes that can quietly accumulate between sessions. Monthly reviews cover the settings that are easy to leave alone too long: recovery options, connected apps, privacy controls, and the accounts that still have access you no longer need. Quarterly reviews are where you step back and inspect the whole system for drift, because security failures often come from gradual neglect rather than one dramatic mistake. The point is not to create a long maintenance ritual. It is to assign each layer of protection a review cycle that matches how quickly it can become stale.

A weekly routine should be short enough to complete without delay. Start by checking recent sign-in activity and any security alerts the platform has sent. If you see a login from an unfamiliar device, location, or browser, investigate immediately instead of assuming it was a glitch. Then review direct messages, comments, and mentions for anything that looks like a request for codes, payment, account verification, or urgent action. This is also the right time to scan for posts that were published while you were distracted or away from the account. For creators and small businesses, that includes checking whether scheduled content went out as intended and whether any replies were made from the correct account. If something looks off, treat it as a signal, not a nuisance.

Weekly checks are also useful for keeping your public face aligned with your actual security posture. Review whether a recent post revealed more than you intended, whether a tagged photo exposes a location you would rather keep private, or whether a comment thread has pulled you into a conversation that should move to a more controlled channel. This is not about becoming fearful of ordinary interaction. It is about noticing when routine engagement starts creating unnecessary exposure. A quick weekly scan helps you catch those small leaks before they become a pattern that others can map.

Monthly maintenance should focus on the parts of the account that attackers often use after the first line of defense fails. Confirm that your password manager is storing current credentials, that multi-factor authentication is still enabled, and that your recovery email and phone number are still yours. Review trusted devices, active sessions, and connected apps, and remove anything you no longer recognize or use. Pay special attention to third-party tools that can post, read messages, or access analytics, since those permissions tend to linger long after the original need has passed. Consumer data collection and surveillance practices make it easier for private information to circulate beyond the original context [260], so reducing unnecessary access is not just housekeeping; it is exposure control.

Once a month, also inspect your privacy settings with a practical question in mind: who can reach me, who can identify me, and what can they infer from the account if they look closely? That means revisiting audience controls, discovery settings, tagging permissions, and location features, especially after app updates or platform redesigns. Social apps often change defaults in ways that are easy to miss, and a setting that was once private can become broader after a refresh or a new feature rollout. If you manage a business or creator account, use the monthly review to confirm that team access is still appropriate and that people who no longer need entry have been removed. Shared access becomes safer only when it is actively maintained.

Quarterly reviews should be more deliberate. This is the time to step back and map the account as a system rather than a collection of settings. Ask which platforms are still essential, which connected services are still active, and which workflows have quietly merged in ways that make recovery harder. If you use the same phone, email address, or browser profile for personal and professional activity, note where that overlap increases the blast radius of a compromise. A quarterly review is also a good point to test your recovery process: make sure backup codes are stored securely, verify that you can still reach your recovery methods, and confirm that the people or staff who need access actually know what to do in an emergency. Research on cybersecurity risk management emphasizes that useful programs reduce uncertainty by clarifying what matters and how it is controlled [264]. A quarterly inspection does exactly that.

For individuals, the routine can stay compact: weekly sign-in and message checks, monthly account and privacy reviews, quarterly recovery and device audits. For influencers and small teams, add one more layer of discipline: assign responsibility. Someone should know who checks security alerts, who reviews connected tools, and who verifies that public-facing accounts still match the approved brand voice. Control only works when the people involved understand their role and can act on it consistently [111]. If more than one person touches the account, a routine that is clear and repeatable matters even more, because confusion about who is supposed to notice a problem is one of the easiest ways for a warning sign to be missed.

The routine should also be realistic enough to survive busy periods. A security habit that takes an hour every week is more likely to be skipped than one that takes ten focused minutes and a monthly deeper review. Keep a short checklist in the same place every time, and use the same order so nothing is forgotten. If you prefer, group the checks by question: Is anyone in the account who should not be there? Has anything changed in the settings that affect visibility or recovery? Does the public profile still match the level of exposure I intend? Repeating the same questions over time makes it easier to notice drift, and drift is often what turns an ordinary account into an easy target.

Checklists for individuals, influencers, and small teams

For individuals, the checklist should be short enough to use without hesitation and specific enough to catch the weak points that matter most. Start with the account itself: confirm that the password is unique, stored in a password manager, and not reused anywhere else. Make sure multi-factor authentication is turned on, and verify that the recovery email and phone number still belong to you. Review active sessions, logged-in devices, and connected apps at least once a month, and remove anything you do not recognize or no longer use. If the platform offers login alerts, keep them enabled and treat every unexpected sign-in notice as a real signal until you verify it. Security works best when these checks become routine rather than something you do only after a scare [151].

The next layer is what your account reveals by default. Review who can see your posts, stories, friend list, and profile details, then narrow those audiences wherever the platform allows it. Turn off contact syncing if you do not need it, limit discoverability through phone number and email lookups, and be deliberate about location sharing and tagging permissions. A profile that is easy to find is not automatically unsafe, but a profile that is easy to map becomes easier to exploit. Keep in mind that privacy controls are not just about hiding content; they are about reducing the amount of context an attacker can assemble from ordinary behavior [272].

Use a simple posting rule: if a post reveals where you are, when you are away, who you are with, or what you are about to do, pause before sharing it publicly. That does not mean you cannot post personal content. It means you should separate immediate sharing from safe sharing. Many people are better served by posting after an event rather than during it, especially when travel, routines, family details, or workplace information are involved. The same rule applies to comments and replies. A casual response can expose more than the original post because it confirms relationships, schedules, and habits that were not obvious at first glance.

For influencers, the checklist needs to cover both account control and audience trust. Confirm that the main profile, the recovery channels, and any monetization or brand-deal accounts are protected with strong authentication and current contact information. Review whether assistants, editors, agencies, or managers have access that is still necessary, and remove stale permissions without delay. If you use scheduling tools, analytics apps, link-in-bio services, or browser extensions, verify that each one is legitimate, still needed, and limited to the smallest set of permissions possible. In creator environments, third-party tools often become the easiest path into a high-value account because they sit close to publishing and messaging functions [269].

Influencers should also maintain a public-facing consistency check. Compare your display name, handle, profile image, bio, and visual style across platforms so followers can recognize the real account quickly. That consistency makes impersonation harder to pull off and easier for your audience to spot. If you sell products, promote services, or direct people to payment pages, test those links regularly and make sure they still point to the correct destination. A broken or hijacked link can damage trust even when the account itself remains secure. It is also wise to keep a brief internal record of your standard posting voice, common calls to action, and approved brand language so that a compromise or impersonation attempt stands out faster.

For small teams, the checklist has to account for shared responsibility without creating confusion about who owns what. Every team should know which accounts are core assets, who has administrative access, how access is approved, and how it is removed when someone changes roles. Shared inboxes, ad accounts, scheduling platforms, and cloud folders should be reviewed on a fixed schedule, not only when someone remembers to check them. The simplest rule is to limit access by job need and to avoid giving full control when a narrower permission will do. In practice, that means separating publishing, billing, analytics, and recovery access whenever the platform allows it [46].

A small team also needs a written response path for routine problems. Decide in advance who handles suspicious DMs, who verifies brand requests, who can approve password resets, and who speaks publicly if an account is compromised. Keep backup codes and recovery details in a secure place that more than one trusted person can reach if necessary, but not in a shared document that everyone can edit. Review device security as part of the same checklist: updates installed, screen locks enabled, work apps removed from old devices, and public or shared devices avoided for admin tasks. If the team uses bring-your-own-device practices, make sure the same security standards apply whether the device is personal or company-owned [271].

The most useful team checklist is the one that can be completed quickly and repeated often. A weekly pass might cover logins, alerts, messages, and pending requests. A monthly pass might cover passwords, recovery settings, connected tools, and access lists. A quarterly pass might cover audience settings, link destinations, content permissions, and who still needs administrative rights. The goal is not to create a burden that people ignore. It is to make the right actions easy enough that they happen before a problem becomes public. When the checklist is built around real roles and real workflows, it stops being paperwork and becomes part of how the account stays safe.

Teaching family members or staff to follow the same standards

Teaching family members or staff to follow the same standards works best when the rules are few, specific, and visible. People do not fail security because they reject it in principle; they fail because they are busy, distracted, or unsure which rule matters in the moment. If one person in a household or team treats direct messages casually, reuses passwords, or approves apps without checking, that weakness can spread to everyone else. A shared standard is important because social media incidents rarely stay isolated. One compromised account can be used to reach relatives, coworkers, customers, and contacts who assume the message is legitimate. Phishing remains one of the most common ways attackers gain access, and its effects often include financial loss, identity theft, and reputational damage [273].

Start by turning security expectations into plain language that anyone can repeat. Instead of a long policy document, define the nonnegotiables: use unique passwords stored in a password manager, turn on multi-factor authentication, never share one-time codes, verify unexpected requests through a separate channel, and report suspicious activity immediately. If the person you are training cannot explain the rule back to you in one sentence, it is probably too complicated. The goal is not to make everyone sound technical. The goal is to make the right action the easy action. NIST guidance on basic information security emphasizes the value of clear procedures, least privilege, and consistent user practices rather than relying on memory or good intentions alone [151].

It also helps to assign roles based on responsibility, not confidence. In a family setting, one adult may manage recovery emails and backup codes, while another handles device updates and checking account alerts. In a small business or creator team, one person may approve public posts, another may review connected apps, and a third may monitor login notifications. The point is to avoid assuming that "someone else" is watching. Shared access should always be limited to what is actually needed. If a family member or employee only needs to post content, they should not also have access to billing, recovery settings, or the primary email account unless that access is necessary and documented.

Training works better when it uses examples from the platforms people already use. Show what a fake support message looks like, how an impersonation account may copy a profile photo or display name, and why urgency is a warning sign rather than a reason to act quickly. Then practice the response: pause, verify outside the platform, and ask a second person if the request involves money, codes, login links, or account changes. This matters because attackers often rely on pressure and familiarity to bypass judgment. A person who has rehearsed the response is less likely to panic when a real message arrives. For creators and staff, that rehearsal should include brand-specific risks such as fake partnership offers, invoice scams, and requests to “confirm” login details.

Written rules should be short enough to keep near the workspace or saved in a shared note. A one-page standard might include what counts as an urgent request, which accounts are off-limits for sharing, how often passwords and recovery methods are reviewed, and who to contact if something looks wrong. Make the escalation path obvious: if a family member sees a suspicious login alert, they should know whether to call, text, or message a designated person immediately. If a staff member receives a strange brand inquiry, they should know whether to ignore it, save evidence, or route it to a manager. The faster the response path is understood, the less room an attacker has to exploit hesitation.

Regular check-ins matter because standards drift when no one revisits them. A monthly five-minute review is often enough to catch problems before they spread: is multi-factor authentication still on, are recovery details still current, have any new apps been connected, and has anyone received a suspicious message recently? This kind of routine reinforces the idea that security is normal maintenance, not a punishment after something goes wrong. It also gives you a chance to correct habits gently before they harden into risk. If someone keeps clicking links from unknown senders or ignoring login alerts, the answer is not just more warnings. It is clearer instruction, a simpler process, and, when needed, tighter access.

Finally, model the behavior you want others to copy. People are much more likely to follow a standard they see used consistently than one they hear about only after a mistake. If you want family members or staff to verify messages before acting, do that yourself. If you want them to avoid sharing passwords, never ask for exceptions. If you want them to report suspicious activity quickly, respond without blame when they do. That kind of consistency builds trust, and trust makes security easier to sustain. In practice, the strongest shared standard is not the most detailed one; it is the one that people actually use when the platform is noisy, the request is urgent, and the safer choice is not the most convenient one.

Measuring progress and keeping security practical instead of overwhelming

Security stays manageable when you measure a few meaningful things instead of trying to track everything. The goal is not to create a dashboard that looks impressive; it is to know whether the protections you set up are actually reducing risk. In practice, that means choosing indicators that are easy to check, hard to fake, and tied to outcomes you care about: fewer surprise logins, fewer risky permissions, fewer public exposures, and faster recovery when something does go wrong. A security routine becomes practical when it answers a simple question: Are we safer than we were last month, and can we prove it without spending hours on the answer?

One useful measure is the number of high-risk gaps that remain open. That includes obvious items such as multi-factor authentication not being enabled, recovery information that no longer belongs to you, old connected apps with broad access, or public profile details that reveal more than necessary. Another is the amount of time those gaps stay open. A missing setting is a problem; a missing setting that sits untouched for months is a pattern. The difference matters because security is often lost through delay, not ignorance. People usually know they should fix a weak spot. What they need is a way to notice whether they are actually closing it before it becomes the easiest path in.

It also helps to measure how quickly you notice something unusual. If a login alert, strange message, or unexpected profile change takes days to catch, the issue is not only the event itself but the lag in detection. Faster detection gives you more options and less damage. You do not need a formal incident-management system to benefit from this idea. You can simply ask whether your alerts are turned on, whether you check them, and whether you know what "normal" looks like for your own account. Research on cybersecurity behavior consistently shows that people do better when security is framed as a workable habit rather than a blame exercise [248]. That same logic applies here: measure the habits you can repeat, not the perfection you cannot maintain.

Another practical measure is the number of unnecessary connections you remove. Over time, social accounts accumulate access points: old phone numbers, shared passwords, inactive devices, temporary collaborators, automation tools, browser extensions, and apps you barely remember approving. Each one adds maintenance burden and potential exposure. If you review those connections on a regular schedule, you can track whether your environment is getting cleaner or more cluttered. A smaller, better-understood set of trusted tools is usually safer than a sprawling setup that no one fully remembers how to audit. This is especially important for creators and small businesses, where convenience tools often become permanent even after the original need has passed.

To keep the process from becoming overwhelming, use a simple tiered approach. Some items deserve frequent attention because they can change quickly: new login alerts, unfamiliar messages, follower spikes, and permission requests. Others can be reviewed less often: recovery settings, privacy defaults, connected apps, and device inventory. A third group only needs occasional review: whether your public bio still reflects what you want exposed, whether your backup codes are stored safely, and whether your account structure still matches your current role. Keeping the cadence different for each type of control prevents the common mistake of treating every security task as equally urgent. That mistake is what makes people stop checking altogether.

It is also useful to measure friction. If a safety step is so complicated that you avoid it, the control may be technically strong but operationally weak. Good security should slow an attacker more than it slows you. If you find yourself repeatedly skipping a step because it takes too long, that is a signal to simplify the process, not abandon the protection. For example, if a review requires too many logins or too much searching to complete, you may need a checklist, a password manager, or a clearer division between personal and business accounts. Security works best when it fits the way people actually behave, which is why human-centered approaches are increasingly emphasized in cybersecurity research [248].

For individuals, the easiest way to keep score is with a short monthly record. Note whether multi-factor authentication is on, whether recovery details are current, whether any new devices or apps were approved, whether there were any suspicious messages or login alerts, and whether you removed anything outdated. For influencers and small teams, add one more layer: who has access, what tools can post on your behalf, and whether the approval process for public content is still being followed. The point is not to generate paperwork. It is to make progress visible. When you can see that the number of open risks is shrinking, the review cycle becomes encouraging instead of exhausting. When the list starts growing again, you catch the drift early enough to correct it before it turns into a larger problem.

Progress in social media security is rarely dramatic. It looks like fewer weak links, fewer surprises, and fewer decisions made under pressure. If you keep the metrics small, the routine realistic, and the review regular, security stops feeling like a special project and starts functioning as part of normal account maintenance. That is the threshold you want: enough structure to stay protected, not so much complexity that the system collapses under its own weight.

Citations

The following sources were referenced in the preceding chapters. Each entry links back to the inline reference in the text. All sources were verified against the OpenAlex academic database at the time of generation.

Adil Rasheed, Omer San, Trond Kvamsdal (2020). Digital Twin: Values, Challenges and Enablers From a Modeling Perspective . https://doi.org/10.1109/access.2020.2970143 Mark Chen, Jerry Tworek, Heewoo Jun et al. (2021). Evaluating Large Language Models Trained on Code . https://doi.org/10.48550/arxiv.2107.03374 Maria Stoyanova, Yannis Nikoloudakis, Spyros Panagiotakis et al. (2020). A Survey on the Internet of Things (IoT) Forensics: Challenges, Approaches, and Open Issues . https://doi.org/10.1109/comst.2019.2962586 Robert Chesney, Danielle Keats Citron (2018). Deep Fakes: A Looming Challenge for Privacy, Democracy, and National Security . https://doi.org/10.2139/ssrn.3213954 Miles Brundage, Shahar Avin, Jack Clark et al. (2018). The malicious use of artificial intelligence: Forecasting, prevention, and mitigation . https://doi.org/10.17863/cam.22520 Dimitrios Buhalis, Tracy Harwood, Vanja Bogicevic et al. (2019). Technological disruptions in services: lessons from tourism and hospitality . https://doi.org/10.1108/josm-12-2018-0398 Sahami, Mehran, Roach, Steve, Cuadros-Vargas, Ernesto et al. (2013). Computer Science Curricula 2013: Curriculum Guidelines for Undergraduate Degree Programs in Computer Science . https://doi.org/10.1145/2534860 Nadeem Ahmed, Regio A. Michelin, Wanli Xue et al. (2020). A Survey of COVID-19 Contact Tracing Apps .

https://doi.org/10.1109/access.2020.3010226 Huw Roberts, Josh Cowls, Jessica Morley et al. (2020). The Chinese approach to artificial intelligence: an analysis of policy, ethics, and regulation . https://doi.org/10.1007/s00146-020-00992-2 Joshua A. Tucker, Andrew M. Guess, Pablo Barberá et al. (2018). Social Media, Political Polarization, and Political Disinformation: A Review of the Scientific Literature . https://doi.org/10.2139/ssrn.3144139 Harjinder Singh Lallie, Lynsay A. Shepherd, Jason R. C. Nurse et al. (2021). Cyber security in the age of COVID-19: A timeline and analysis of cyber-crime and cyber-attacks during the pandemic . https://doi.org/10.1016/j.cose.2021.102248 Krzysztof Wach, Cong Doanh Duong, Joanna Ejdys et al. (2023). The dark side of generative artificial intelligence: A critical analysis of controversies and risks of ChatGPT . https://doi.org/10.15678/eber.2023.110201 Lubna Luxmi Dhirani, Noorain Mukhtiar, Bhawani Shankar Chowdhry et al. (2023). Ethical Dilemmas and Privacy Issues in Emerging Technologies: A Review . https://doi.org/10.3390/s23031151 Hossein Hassani, Christina Beneki, Stephan Unger et al. (2020). Text Mining in Big Data Analytics . https://doi.org/10.3390/bdcc4010001 Nan Sun, Ming Ding, Jiaojiao Jiang et al. (2023). Cyber Threat Intelligence Mining for Proactive Cybersecurity Defense: A Survey and New Perspectives . https://doi.org/10.1109/comst.2023.3273282 Joachim Bjørge Ulven, Gaute Wangen (2021). A Systematic Review of Cybersecurity Risks in Higher Education . https://doi.org/10.3390/fi13020039 Ioannis Agrafiotis, Jason R. C. Nurse, Michael Goldsmith et al. (2018). A taxonomy of cyber-harms: Defining the impacts of cyber-attacks and understanding how they propagate . https://doi.org/10.1093/cybsec/tyy006 Pawani Porambage, Gürkan Gür, Diana Pamela Moya Osorio et al. (2021). The Roadmap to 6G Security and Privacy . https://doi.org/10.1109/ojcoms.2021.3078081 Bader Alouffi, Muhammad Hasnain, Abdullah Alharbi et al. (2021). A Systematic Literature Review on Cloud Computing Security: Threats and Mitigation Strategies . https://doi.org/10.1109/access.2021.3073203 Jean-Paul A. Yaacoub, Hassan Noura, Ola Salman et al. (2021). Robotics cyber security: vulnerabilities, attacks, countermeasures, and recommendations . https://doi.org/10.1007/s10207-021-00545-8 Neetesh Saxena, Emma Hayes, Elisa Bertino et al. (2020). Impact and Key Challenges of Insider Threats on Organizations and Critical Businesses . https://doi.org/10.3390/electronics9091460 Florian Skopik, Tímea Páhi (2020). Under false flag: using technical artifacts for cyber attack attribution . https://doi.org/10.1186/s42400-020-00048-4 Thulfiqar Jabar, Manmeet Mahinderjit Singh (2022). Exploration of Mobile Device Behavior for Mitigating Advanced Persistent Threats (APT): A Systematic Literature Review and Conceptual Framework . https://doi.org/10.3390/s22134662 Michele Campobasso, Luca Allodi (2020). Impersonation-as-a-Service: Characterizing the Emerging Criminal Infrastructure for User Impersonation at Scale . https://doi.org/10.1145/3372297.3417892 Penny Jorna, Russell Smith (2018). Identity crime and misuse in Australia 2017 . https://doi.org/10.52922/sr227198 Daniela Pöhn, Wolfgang Hommel (2023). Towards an Improved Taxonomy of Attacks Related to Digital Identities and Identity Management Systems . https://doi.org/10.1155/2023/5573310 Mohammad Z. Aloudat, Mahmoud Barhamgi, Elias Yaacoub et al. (2025). Security in Metaverse Markets: Challenges and Solutions—A Comprehensive Review . https://doi.org/10.1111/exsy.70094 Matipa Ricky Ngandu, Gardner Mwansa, Ziyanda Mkabe (2025). Strengthening cybersecurity in a government department by addressing password management challenges and human factor vulnerabilities . https://doi.org/10.1007/s10791-025-09659-2 Jhon Melendez, Jomark Noriega, Jose Tiznado et al. (2024). Sectrabank Model to Mitigate Computer Fraud in Electronic Operations through Banking Applications on Android Devices . https://doi.org/10.20944/preprints202404.0238.v1

Guma Ali, Otim Emmanuel, Maad M. Mijwil et al. (2026). A Survey on Securing Smart Finance using Artificial Intelligence and Blockchain . https://doi.org/10.70470/shifra/2026/001 Yogesh K. Dwivedi, Nir Kshetri, Laurie Hughes et al. (2023). Exploring the Darkverse: A Multi-Perspective Analysis of the Negative Societal Impacts of the Metaverse . https://doi.org/10.1007/s10796-023-10400-x Tarana Singh, Arun Solanki, Sanjay Kumar Sharma et al. (2022). A Decade Review on Smart Cities: Paradigms, Challenges and Opportunities . https://doi.org/10.1109/access.2022.3184710 Maha Charfeddine, Habib M. Kammoun, Bechir Hamdaoui et al. (2024). ChatGPT's Security Risks and Benefits: Offensive and Defensive Use-Cases, Mitigation Measures, and Future Implications . https://doi.org/10.1109/access.2024.3367792 Andreas Reis, Rohit Malpani, Effy Vayena et al. (2021). ETHICS AND GOVERNANCE OF ARTIFICIAL INTELLIGENCE FOR HEALTH:WHO GUIDANCE . https://openalex.org/W4412255553 Sonia Katyal (2020). Private Accountability in an Age of Artificial Intelligence . https://doi.org/10.1017/9781108680844.004 Peter K. Yu (2019). The Algorithmic Divide and Equality in the Age of Artificial Intelligence . https://openalex.org/W2981795565 Vanessa Ceia, Benji Nothwehr, Liz Wagner (2021). Gender and Technology: A rights-based and intersectional analysis of key trends . https://doi.org/10.21201/2021.7598 R. V. Gundur, Michael Levi, Volkan Topalli et al. (2021). Evaluating Criminal Transactional Methods in Cyberspace as Understood in an International Context . https://doi.org/10.21428/cb6ab371.5f335e6f Caitlin C. Corrigan, Simon Atuah Asakipaam, Jerry John Kponyo et al. (2023). AI Ethics in Higher Education: Insights from Africa and Beyond . https://doi.org/10.1007/978-3-031-23035-6 Janne J. Olin, Miloš N. Mladenović (2022). Imaginaries of Road Transport Automation in Finnish Governance Culture—A Critical Discourse Analysis . https://doi.org/10.3390/su14031437 Danielle Keats Citron

(2010). Mainstreaming Privacy Torts . https://doi.org/10.15779/z38dm7w Junaid Haseeb (2023). Deception-Based Security Framework for IoT: An Empirical Study . https://doi.org/10.26686/wgtn.21965195 Sathishkumar P, S Chandrakala, P Baraninishanth et al. (2025). SafeTrace – Visualizing and Protecting the Digital Identity of Everyday Internet Users . https://doi.org/10.36948/ijfmr.2025.v07i06.58173 Muhammad Rawish Siddiqui (2025). Big Data and Great Privacy Challenges in the Digital Era - A Comprehensive Study . https://doi.org/10.70844/ijas.2025.2.42 Luyi Sun, Wei Xu, Zaifeng Gao (2026). A Human-Centered Privacy (HCP) Approach to AI . https://doi.org/10.1007/978-981-97-8440-0_116-1 Mohammad Tahaei, Alisa Frik, Kami Vaniea (2021). Privacy Champions in Software Teams: Understanding Their Motivations, Strategies, and Challenges . https://doi.org/10.1145/3411764.3445768 Josephine Wolff (2022). Cyberinsurance Policy . https://doi.org/10.7551/mitpress/13665.001.0001 Harold Abelson, Ross Anderson, Steven M. Bellovin et al. (2024). Bugs in our pockets: the risks of client-side scanning . https://doi.org/10.1093/cybsec/tyad020 Andrea Carson, Liam Fallon (2021). Fighting Fake News: A Study of Online Misinformation Regulation in the Asia Pacific . https://doi.org/10.26181/60640ea43558f Florian Mathis, Kami Vaniea, Mohamed Khamis (2021). Prototyping Usable Privacy and Security Systems: Insights from Experts . https://doi.org/10.1080/10447318.2021.1949134 Priya Kumar, Fiona O'Connell, Li Lucy et al. (2023). Understanding Research Related to Designing for Children's Privacy and Security: A Document Analysis . https://doi.org/10.1145/3585088.3589375 Amy Winecoff, Elizabeth Anne Watkins (2022). Artificial Concepts of Artificial Intelligence . https://doi.org/10.1145/3514094.3534138 Malcolm W. Harkins (2013). Managing Risk and Information Security . https://doi.org/10.1007/978-1-4302-5114-9 Shivani Gaba, Haneef Khan, Khalid J Almalki et al. (2023). Holochain: An Agent-Centric Distributed Hash Table Security in Smart IoT

Applications . https://doi.org/10.1109/access.2023.3300220 Malcolm W. Harkins (2012). Managing Risk and Information Security: Protect to Enable . https://doi.org/10.1007/978-1-4302-5114-9 Rabia Khan, Pardeep Kumar, Dushantha Nalin K. Jayakody et al. (2019). A Survey on Security and Privacy of 5G Technologies: Potential Solutions, Recent Advancements, and Future Directions . https://doi.org/10.1109/comst.2019.2933899 Paula Fraga-Lamas, Tiago M. Fernández-Caramés (2019). A Review on Blockchain Technologies for an Advanced and Cyber-Resilient Automotive Industry . https://doi.org/10.1109/access.2019.2895302 Bako Ali, Ali Ismail Awad (2018). Cyber and Physical Security Vulnerability Assessment for IoT-Based Smart Homes . https://doi.org/10.3390/s18030817 Ilona Kickbusch, Dario Piselli, Anurag Agrawal et al. (2021). The Lancet and Financial Times Commission on governing health futures 2030: growing up in a digital world . https://doi.org/10.1016/s0140-6736(21)01824-9 Joe Abou Jaoude, Raafat George Saadé (2019). Blockchain Applications – Usage in Different Domains . https://doi.org/10.1109/access.2019.2902501 Thomas C. King, Nikita Aggarwal, Mariarosaria Taddeo et al. (2019). Artificial Intelligence Crime: An Interdisciplinary Analysis of Foreseeable Threats and Solutions . https://doi.org/10.1007/s11948-018-00081-0 Arash Heidari, Nima Jafari Navimipour, Hasan Dağ et al. (2023). Deepfake detection using deep learning methods: A systematic and comprehensive review . https://doi.org/10.1002/widm.1520 Firoj Parwej, Syed Qamar Abbas, Jai Pratap Dixit et al. (2021). A Systematic Literature Review on the Cyber Security . https://doi.org/10.18535/ijsrm/v9i12.ec04 Tance Suleski, Mohiuddin Ahmed, Wencheng Yang et al. (2023). A review of multi-factor authentication in the Internet of Healthcare Things . https://doi.org/10.1177/20552076231177144 Mohammed Ali Al-Garadi, Amr Mohamed, Abdulla Al-Ali et al. (2020). A Survey of Machine and Deep Learning Methods for Internet of Things (IoT) Security . https://doi.org/

10.1109/comst.2020.2988293 Amani S. Ibrahim, Dhananjay Thiruvady, Jean-Guy Schneider et al. (2020). The Challenges of Leveraging Threat Intelligence to Stop Data Breaches . https://doi.org/10.3389/fcomp.2020.00036 Mohammed Ali Al-Garadi, Amr Mohamed, Abdulla Al-Ali et al. (2018). A Survey of Machine and Deep Learning Methods for Internet of Things\n (IoT) Security . https://doi.org/10.48550/arxiv.1807.11023 Zhen Guo, Jin-Hee Cho, Ing-Ray Chen et al. (2020). Online Social Deception and Its Countermeasures: A Survey . https://doi.org/10.1109/access.2020.3047337 Jide Edu, José M. Such, Guillermo Suárez-Tangil (2019). Smart Home Personal Assistants: A Security and Privacy Review . https://doi.org/10.48550/arxiv.1903.05593 Steven Feldstein (2021). The road to digital unfreedom: how artificial intelligence is reshaping repression . https://doi.org/10.24923/2305-8757.2021-5.4 Mekhail Mustak, Joni Salminen, Matti Mäntymäki et al. (2022). Deepfakes: Deceptions, mitigations, and opportunities . https://doi.org/10.1016/j.jbusres.2022.113368 Danielle Caled, Mário J. Silva (2021). Digital media and misinformation: An outlook on multidisciplinary strategies against manipulation . https://doi.org/10.1007/s42001-021-00118-8 Gajendra Liyanaarachchi, Matthieu Mifsud, Giampaolo Viglia (2024). Virtual influencers and data privacy: Introducing the multi-privacy paradox . https://doi.org/10.1016/j.jbusres.2024.114584 Muzammil Hussain, Philip N. Howard (2013). State Power 2.0: Authoritarian Entrenchment and Political Engagement Worldwide . https://openalex.org/W396128684 Leonie Maria Tanczer, Ronald J. Deibert, Didier Bigo et al. (2019). Online Surveillance, Censorship, and Encryption in Academia . https://doi.org/10.1093/isp/ekz016 Michel van Eeten, Milton Mueller, N. van Eijk (2014). The Internet and the State: A Survey of Key Developments . https://openalex.org/W2258641370 Lawrence J. Trautman (2020). GOVERNANCE OF THE FACEBOOK PRIVACY CRISIS . https://doi.org/10.5195/tlp.2020.234 Tony Roberts,

Judy Gitahi, Patrick Allam et al. (2023). Mapping the Supply of Surveillance Technologies to Africa: Case Studies from Nigeria, Ghana, Morocco, Malawi, and Zambia . https://doi.org/10.19088/ids.2023.027 Oghenekome Urefe, Theodore Narku Odonkor, Shadrack Obeng et al. (2024). Innovative strategic marketing practices to propel small business development and competitiveness . https://doi.org/10.30574/msarr.2024.11.2.0122 Baqer Khudair Al-Hadrawi (2024). Mind Intruders: Psychological, Legal, and Social Effects of Human Parasites in the Age of Technological Progress . https://doi.org/10.57239/pjlss-2024-22.2.00414 Sara Quach, Park Thaichon, Kelly D. Martin et al. (2022). Digital technologies: tensions in privacy and data . https://doi.org/10.1007/s11747-022-00845-y Yuntao Wang, Yanghe Pan, Miao Yan et al. (2023). A Survey on ChatGPT: AI–Generated Contents, Challenges, and Solutions . https://doi.org/10.1109/ojcs.2023.3300321 Frank Cremer, Barry Sheehan, Michael Fortmann et al. (2022). Cyber risk and cybersecurity: a systematic review of data availability . https://doi.org/10.1057/s41288-022-00266-6 David Eckhoff, Isabel Wagner (2017). Privacy in the Smart City—Applications, Technologies, Challenges, and Solutions . https://doi.org/10.1109/comst.2017.2748998 Nicola Capuano, Giuseppe Fenza, Vincenzo Loia et al. (2022). Explainable Artificial Intelligence in CyberSecurity: A Survey . https://doi.org/10.1109/access.2022.3204171 Naeem Syed, Syed Wajid Ali Shah, Arash Shaghaghi et al. (2022). Zero Trust Architecture (ZTA): A Comprehensive Survey . https://doi.org/10.1109/access.2022.3174679 Nickson M. Karie, Nor Masri Sahri, Wencheng Yang et al. (2021). A Review of Security Standards and Frameworks for IoT-Based Smart Environments . https://doi.org/10.1109/access.2021.3109886 Ali Farazmand (2022). Global Encyclopedia of Public Administration, Public Policy, and Governance . https://doi.org/10.1007/978-3-030-66252-3 Abdullahi Chowdhury, Gour Karmakar,

Joarder Kamruzzaman et al. (2020). Attacks on Self-Driving Cars and Their Countermeasures: A Survey . https://doi.org/10.1109/access.2020.3037705 Cecilia Ka Yuk Chan, Tom Colloton (2024). Generative AI in Higher Education . https://doi.org/10.4324/9781003459026 Scott Shackelford (2009). From Nuclear War to Net War: Analogizing Cyber Attacks in International Law . https://doi.org/10.15779/z38ks9b Edward Griffor, Chris L. Greer, David A. Wollman et al. (2017). Framework for cyber-physical systems: volume 2, working group reports . https://doi.org/10.6028/nist.sp.1500-202 Pintu Kumar Sadhu, Venkata P. Yanambaka, Ahmed Abdelgawad et al. (2022). Prospect of Internet of Medical Things: A Review on Security Requirements and Solutions . https://doi.org/10.3390/s22155517 Zheng Xiang, Matthias Fuchs, Ulrike Gretzel et al. (2020). Handbook of e-Tourism . https://doi.org/10.1007/978-3-030-05324-6 Senthil Kumar Jagatheesaperumal, Quoc-Viet Pham, Rukhsana Ruby et al. (2022). Explainable AI Over the Internet of Things (IoT): Overview, State-of-the-Art and Future Directions . https://doi.org/10.1109/ojcoms.2022.3215676 Arjen Boin, Magnus Ekengren, Mark Rhinard (2021). Understanding the Creeping Crisis . https://doi.org/10.1007/978-3-030-70692-0 Guma Ali, Maad M. Mıjwıl, Bosco Apparatus Buruga et al. (2024). A Survey on Artificial Intelligence in Cybersecurity for Smart Agriculture: State-of-the-Art, Cyber Threats, Artificial Intelligence Applications, and Ethical Concerns . https://doi.org/10.58496/mjcsc/2024/007 Shaharyar Khan, Ilya Kabanov, Yunke Hua et al. (2022). A Systematic Analysis of the Capital One Data Breach: Critical Lessons Learned . https://doi.org/10.1145/3546068 Dan Hendrycks, Mantas Mazeika, Thomas Woodside (2023). An Overview of Catastrophic AI Risks . https://doi.org/10.48550/arxiv.2306.12001 Amy L. Stein (2020). Artificial Intelligence and Climate Change . https://openalex.org/W3046424788 Gabriela Viale Pereira, Elsa Estévez, Diego Cardona et al. (2020). South American

Expert Roundtable: Increasing Adaptive Governance Capacity for Coping with Unintended Side Effects of Digital Transformation . https://doi.org/10.3390/su12020718 Martin Strohmeier (2016). Security in Next Generation Air Traffic Communication Networks . https://doi.org/10.13140/rg.2.2.21924.48006 Michaël Friedewald, J. Peter Burgess, Johann Čas et al. (2017). Surveillance, Privacy and Security . https://doi.org/10.4324/9781315619309 Linnet Taylor, Gargi Sharma, Aaron Martin et al. (2020). Data justice and COVID-19 : Global perspectives . https://openalex.org/W3048965658 John Crawford, Lev Menand, Morgan Ricks (2021). FedAccounts: Digital Dollars . https://openalex.org/W3196947385 Elias Wright (2019). The Future of Facial Recognition Is Not Fully Known: Developing Privacy and Security Regulatory Mechanisms for Facial Recognition in the Retail Sector . https://openalex.org/W2924840180 Shah Rukh, Stanley Tochukwu Oziri, Omorinsola Bibire Seyi-Lande (2025). A framework for leveraging artificial intelligence in strategic business decision-making . https://doi.org/10.51594/gjabr.v3i11.171 Mehtab Khan, Alex Hanna (2022). The Subjects and Stages of AI Dataset Development: A Framework for Dataset Accountability . https://doi.org/10.2139/ssrn.4217148 World Bank (2020). Philippines Digital Economy Report 2020 . https://doi.org/10.1596/34606 Dan Blum (2020). Rational Cybersecurity for Business . https://doi.org/10.1007/978-1-4842-5952-8 Stephen McCarthy, Paidi O'Raghallaigh, Yuzhu Li et al. (2023). Control enactment in context: Understanding the interaction of controlee and controller perceptions in inter-organisational project teams . https://doi.org/10.1111/isj.12434 Dan Blum (2020). Rational Cybersecurity for Business: The Security Leaders' Guide to Business Alignment . https://doi.org/10.1007/978-1-4842-5952-8 Jayesh Rane, Reshma Amol Chaudhari, Nitin Liladhar Rane (2025). Enhancing Sustainable Supply Chain Resilience Through Artificial Intelligence and Machine Learning:

Industry 4.0 and Industry 5.0 in Manufacturing . https://doi.org/10.70593/978-93-7185-621-8 Pankaj Khatiwada, Bian Yang, Jia-Chun Lin et al. (2024). Patient-Generated Health Data (PGHD): Understanding, Requirements, Challenges, and Existing Techniques for Data Security and Privacy . https://doi.org/10.3390/jpm14030282 Ansgar Koene, Chris Clifton, Yohko Hatada et al. (2019). A governance framework for algorithmic accountability and transparency . https://doi.org/10.2861/59990 Welby, Benjamin (2019). The impact of digital government on citizen well-being . https://doi.org/10.1787/24bac82f-en OECD (2020). Digital transformation and the futures of civic space to 2030 . https://doi.org/10.1787/79b34d37-en Yixin Zou, Kaiwen Sun, Tanisha Afnan et al. (2023). Cross-Contextual Examination of Older Adults' Privacy Concerns, Behaviors, and Vulnerabilities . https://doi.org/10.56553/popets-2024-0009 Maia J. Boyd, Jamar L. Sullivan, Marshini Chetty et al. (2021). Understanding the Security and Privacy Advice Given to Black Lives Matter Protesters . https://doi.org/10.1145/3411764.3445061 Richard Heeks (2016). Examining 'Digital Development': The Shape of Things to Come? . https://doi.org/10.2139/ssrn.3431739 World Bank (2020). How Regulators Respond To FinTech . https://doi.org/10.1596/33698 Alessandro Acquisti, Idris Adjerid, Rebecca Balebako et al. (2017). Nudges for Privacy and Security . https://doi.org/10.1145/3054926 Sherali Zeadally, Erwin Adi, Zubair Baig et al. (2020). Harnessing Artificial Intelligence Capabilities to Improve Cybersecurity . https://doi.org/10.1109/access.2020.2968045 Cameron S. D. Brown (2015). Investigating And Prosecuting Cyber Crime: Forensic Dependencies And Barriers To Justice . https://doi.org/10.5281/zenodo.22387 Musa Ndiaye, Stephen S. Oyewobi, Adnan M. Abu-Mahfouz et al. (2020). IoT in the Wake of COVID-19: A Survey on Contributions, Challenges and Evolution . https://doi.org/10.1109/access.2020.3030090 David Buil-Gil, Steven Kemp, Stefanie Kuenzel et al.

(2023). The digital harms of smart home devices: A systematic literature review . https://doi.org/10.1016/j.chb.2023.107770 Natalia Bayona, Hernan Epstein, Dirk Glaesser et al. (2021). Big Data for Better Tourism Policy, Management, and Sustainable Recovery from COVID-19 . https://doi.org/10.22617/spr210438-2 Franklin Allen, Xian Gu, Julapa Jagtiani (2020). A Survey of Fintech Research and Policy Discussion . https://doi.org/10.21799/frbp.wp.2020.21 Randa Basheer, Bassel Alkhatib (2021). Threats from the Dark: A Review over Dark Web Investigation Research for Cyber Threat Intelligence . https://doi.org/10.1155/2021/1302999 Arianna Trozze, Josh Kamps, Eray Arda Akartuna et al. (2022). Cryptocurrencies and future financial crime . https://doi.org/10.1186/s40163-021-00163-8 Meredydd Williams, Jason R. C. Nurse, Sadie Creese (2019). Smartwatch games: Encouraging privacy-protective behaviour in a longitudinal study . https://doi.org/10.1016/j.chb.2019.04.026 Simon Elias Bibri (2023). The Metaverse as a Virtual Model of Platform Urbanism: Its Converging AIoT, XReality, Neurotech, and Nanobiotech and Their Applications, Challenges, and Risks . https://doi.org/10.3390/smartcities6030065 Muyanja-Ssenyonga Jameaba (2024). Digitalization, Emerging Technologies, and Financial Stability: Challenges and Opportunities for the Indonesian Banking Sector and Beyond . https://doi.org/10.2139/ssrn.4808469 Petri Ahokangas, Annabeth Aagaard (2023). The Changing World of Mobile Communications . https://doi.org/10.1007/978-3-031-33191-6 Keir Giles (2023). Russian cyber and information warfare in practice: Lessons observed from the war on Ukraine . https://doi.org/10.55317/9781784135898 Janine S. Hiller (2014). Civil Cyberconflict: Microsoft, Cybercrime, and Botnets . https://openalex.org/W1643670740 Salem Argaw, Juan Ramón Troncoso-Pastoriza, Darren Lacey et al. (2020). Cybersecurity of Hospitals: discussing the challenges and working towards mitigating the risks . https://doi.org/10.1186/

s12911-020-01161-7 Waqas Ahmad, Aamir Rasool, Abdul Rehman Javed et al. (2021). Cyber Security in IoT-Based Cloud Computing: A Comprehensive Survey . https://doi.org/10.3390/electronics11010016 Pardeep Kumar, Yun Lin, Guangdong Bai et al. (2019). Smart Grid Metering Networks: A Survey on Security, Privacy and Open Research Issues . https://doi.org/10.1109/comst.2019.2899354 Muhammad Fakhrul Safitra, Muharman Lubis, Hanif Fakhrurroja (2023). Counterattacking Cyber Threats: A Framework for the Future of Cybersecurity . https://doi.org/10.3390/su151813369 Muhammad Waseem, Muhammad Adnan Khan, Arman Goudarzi et al. (2023). Incorporation of Blockchain Technology for Different Smart Grid Applications: Architecture, Prospects, and Challenges . https://doi.org/10.3390/en16020820 Zia Muhammad, Zahid Anwar, Bilal Saleem et al. (2023). Emerging Cybersecurity and Privacy Threats to Electric Vehicles and Their Impact on Human and Environmental Sustainability . https://doi.org/10.3390/en16031113 Silvio Sampaio, Patrícia R. Sousa, Cristina Martins et al. (2023). Collecting, Processing and Secondary Using Personal and (Pseudo)Anonymized Data in Smart Cities . https://doi.org/10.3390/app13063830 Sunil Chaudhary (2016). The Use of Usable Security and Security Education to Fight Phishing Attacks . https://openalex.org/W2564201078 Basheer Qolomany, Ala Al-Fuqaha, Ajay Gupta et al. (2019). Leveraging Machine Learning and Big Data for Smart Buildings: A Comprehensive Survey . https://doi.org/10.1109/access.2019.2926642 Daniela M. Peluso (2023). The Digital Divide and Futurist Imaginings of Zelle-ous Resistors . https://doi.org/10.17645/si.v11i3.6867 Kenneth S Kurani (2019). User Perceptions of Safety and Security: A Framework for a Transition to Electric-Shared-Automated Vehicles . https://doi.org/10.7922/g2891438 Jyri Rajamäki, Jaakko Helin (2024). The Ethics and Cybersecurity of Artificial Intelligence and Robotics in Helping The Elderly to Manage at Home . https://doi.org/10.3390/info15110729 L

Tiller (2020). Account Recovery Methods for Two-Factor Authentication (2FA): An Exploratory Study . https://doi.org/10.25777/3dhq-pj49 S. Narayana Swamy, Kota Solomon Raju (2020). An Empirical Study on System Level Aspects of Internet of Things (IoT) . https://doi.org/10.1109/access.2020.3029847 Michael Nieles, Kelley Dempsey, Victoria Pillitteri (2017). An introduction to information security . https://doi.org/10.6028/nist.sp.800-12r1 Adegoke Adebukola Adebukola, A. Navya, Foreman Jordan Jordan et al. (2022). Cyber Security as a Threat to Health Care . https://doi.org/10.47941/jts.1149 Rob Kitchin (2016). Getting smarter about smart cities: Improving data privacy and data security . https://openalex.org/W2530835859 Manar Osama, Abdelhamied A. Ateya, Mohammed S. Sayed et al. (2023). Internet of Medical Things and Healthcare 4.0: Trends, Requirements, Challenges, and Research Directions . https://doi.org/10.3390/s23177435 Danial Javaheri, Mahdi Fahmideh, Hassan Chizari et al. (2023). Cybersecurity threats in FinTech: A systematic review . https://doi.org/10.1016/j.eswa.2023.122697 Manpreet Kaur Aiden, Sonia Chhabra, Shweta Mayor Sabharwal et al. (2024). Social Engineering Attacks . https://doi.org/10.1002/9781394230600.ch16 Chukwuka Elendu, Eunice Omeludike, Praise O. Oloyede et al. (2024). Legal implications for clinicians in cybersecurity incidents: A review . https://doi.org/10.1097/md.0000000000039887 Jun Zhang, Dan Tenney (2024). The Evolution of Integrated Advance Persistent Threat and Its Defense Solutions: A Literature Review . https://doi.org/10.4236/ojbm.2024.121021 Cristóbal Cobo Romaní, Pablo Rivera-Vargas (2022). TURN OFF YOUR CAMERA AND TURN ON YOUR PRIVACY A case study about Zoom and digital education in South American countries . https://doi.org/10.31235/osf.io/yanzw Elizabeth Atieno Otieno (2025). Data protection and privacy in e-commerce environment: Systematic review . https://doi.org/10.30574/gscarr.2025.22.1.0024 Michael Hogan, Fang Liu,

Annie W. Sokol et al. (2011). NIST cloud computing standards roadmap : . https://doi.org/10.6028/nist.sp.500-291v1 Boris Otto, Michael ten Hompel, Stefan Wrobel (2022). Designing Data Spaces . https://doi.org/10.1007/978-3-030-93975-5 Utsav Upadhyay, Alok Kumar, Gajanand Sharma et al. (2023). Cyberbullying in the Metaverse . https://doi.org/10.4018/jgim.325793 Stephen A. Matlin, Johanna Hanefeld, Ana Côrte-Real et al. (2024). Digital solutions for migrant and refugee health: a framework for analysis and action . https://doi.org/10.1016/j.lanepe.2024.101190 Sanjay Goel, Brian Nussbaum (2021). Attribution Across Cyber Attack Types: Network Intrusions and Information Operations . https://doi.org/10.1109/ojcoms.2021.3074591 Alia Al Sadawi, Mohamed S. Hassan, Malick Ndiaye (2021). A Survey on the Integration of Blockchain With IoT to Enhance Performance and Eliminate Challenges . https://doi.org/10.1109/access.2021.3070555 Ryan Heartfield, George Loukas, Sanja Budimir et al. (2018). A taxonomy of cyber-physical threats and impact in the smart home . https://doi.org/10.1016/j.cose.2018.07.011 Ons Aouedi, Thai-Hoc Vu, Alessio Sacco et al. (2024). A Survey on Intelligent Internet of Things: Applications, Security, Privacy, and Future Directions . https://doi.org/10.1109/comst.2024.3430368 Joshua Siegel, Dylan C. Erb, Sanjay E. Sarma (2017). A Survey of the Connected Vehicle Landscape—Architectures, Enabling Technologies, Applications, and Development Areas . https://doi.org/10.1109/tits.2017.2749459 Souhila Badra Guendouzi, Samir Ouchani, Hiba EL Assaad et al. (2023). A systematic review of federated learning: Challenges, aggregation methods, and development tools . https://doi.org/10.1016/j.jnca.2023.103714 Raza Nowrozy, Khandakar Ahmed, A. S. M. Kayes et al. (2024). Privacy Preservation of Electronic Health Records in the Modern Era: A Systematic Survey . https://doi.org/10.1145/3653297 Raiha Tallat, Ammar Hawbani, Xingfu Wang et al. (2023). Navigating Industry 5.0: A

Survey of Key Enabling Technologies, Trends, Challenges, and Opportunities . https://doi.org/10.1109/comst.2023.3329472 Abderahman Rejeb, Karim Rejeb, Andrea Appolloni et al. (2023). Unleashing the power of internet of things and blockchain: A comprehensive analysis and future directions . https://doi.org/10.1016/j.iotcps.2023.06.003 Elvira Ismagilova, Laurie Hughes, Nripendra P. Rana et al. (2020). Security, Privacy and Risks Within Smart Cities: Literature Review and Development of a Smart City Interaction Framework . https://doi.org/10.1007/s10796-020-10044-1 Wafaa Kasri, Yassine Himeur, Hamzah Ali Alkhazaleh et al. (2025). From Vulnerability to Defense: The Role of Large Language Models in Enhancing Cybersecurity . https://doi.org/10.3390/computation13020030 Paweł Weichbroth, Kacper Wereszko, Helena Anacka et al. (2023). Security of Cryptocurrencies: A View on the State-of-the-Art Research and Current Developments . https://doi.org/10.3390/s23063155 Melissa Carlton (2016). Development of a Cybersecurity Skills Index: A Scenarios-Based, Hands-On Measure of Non-IT Professionals' Cybersecurity Skills . https://openalex.org/W2548263726 Werner Schroeder (2020). Limits to European Harmonisation of Criminal Law . https://doi.org/10.30709/eucrim-2020-008 Lizzie Coles-Kemp, J.-W. Bullée, Lorena Montoya et al. (2015). Technology-supported Risk Estimation by Predictive Assessment of Socio-technical Security . https://openalex.org/W2794404497 Aran Sam (2022). BALANCING CYBERSECURITY AFTER THE PANDEMIC (Tips and Tricks) . https://doi.org/10.31219/osf.io/4ph8w Tipon Tanchangya, Kamrun Naher, Md Rakib Mia et al. (2025). Assessing the impact of financial technology: Is it a curse or blessing for financial crimes in financial institutions? . https://doi.org/10.18488/89.v11i1.4075 Samuel Hartwig (2020). Frontex: From Coordinating Controls to Combating Crime . https://doi.org/10.30709/eucrim-2020-010 Laith N. AL-Eitan, Haytham Jaouni, Ahmad Mihyar

(2025). Addressing Cyberbiosecurity Challenges in the Modern Era of Biotechnology and Artificial Intelligence . https://doi.org/10.31646/gbio. 282 Alessandro Mantelero, Maria Samantha Esposito (2024). An evidence-based methodology for human rights impact assessment (HRIA) in the development of AI data-intensive systems . https://doi.org/10.1016/j.clsr.2021.105561 Affan Yasin, Rubia Fatima, Zheng JiangBin et al. (2024). Can serious gaming tactics bolster spear-phishing and phishing resilience? : Securing the human hacking in Information Security . https://doi.org/10.1016/j.infsof.2024.107426 Alexander Romanishyn, Olena Malytska, V. A. Goncharuk (2025). AI-driven disinformation: policy recommendations for democratic resilience . https://doi.org/10.3389/frai.2025.1569115 Alexandra Perloff-Giles (2018). Transnational Cyber Offenses: Overcoming Jurisdictional Challenges . https://openalex.org/W2994538853 Imrana Abdullahi Yari, Tobias Dehling, Felix Kluge et al. (2021). Security Engineering of Patient-Centered Health Care Information Systems in Peer-to-Peer Environments: Systematic Review . https://doi.org/10.2196/24460 Abeer Awadallah, Khouloud Eledlebi, Mohamed Jamal Zemerly et al. (2024). Artificial Intelligence-Based Cybersecurity for the Metaverse: Research Challenges and Opportunities . https://doi.org/10.1109/comst. 2024.3442475 Juliana Gómez-Quintero, Shane D. Johnson, Hervé Borrion et al. (2024). A scoping study of crime facilitated by the metaverse . https://doi.org/10.1016/j.futures.2024.103338 Karen Renaud, Merrill Warkentin, Ganna Pogrebna et al. (2023). VISTA: An inclusive insider threat taxonomy, with mitigation strategies . https://doi.org/10.1016/j.im.2023.103877 N. Ravichandran, Tahrhunraj Tewaraja, Vishendraa Rajasegaran et al. (2024). Comprehensive Review Analysis and Countermeasures for Cybersecurity Threats: DDoS, Ransomware, and Trojan Horse Attacks . https://doi.org/10.20944/preprints202409.1369.v1 Juliana Gómez, Shane D. Johnson, Hervé

Borrion et al. (2023). A scoping study of crime facilitated by the metaverse . https://doi.org/10.31235/osf.io/x9vbn Vinden Wylde, Nisha Rawindaran, John Lawrence et al. (2022). Cybersecurity, Data Privacy and Blockchain: A Review . https://doi.org/10.1007/s42979-022-01020-4 Rosana Montañez, Edward J. Golob, Shouhuai Xu (2020). Human Cognition Through the Lens of Social Engineering Cyberattacks . https://doi.org/10.3389/fpsyg.2020.01755 Fran Casino, Eugenia Politou, Efthimios Alepis et al. (2019). Immutability and Decentralized Storage: An Analysis of Emerging Threats . https://doi.org/10.1109/access.2019.2962017 Abderahman Rejeb, Karim Rejeb, Steven J. Simske et al. (2021). Blockchain technology in the smart city: a bibliometric review . https://doi.org/10.1007/s11135-021-01251-2 Ala Mughaid, Shadi AlZu'bi, Adnan A. Hnaif et al. (2022). An intelligent cyber security phishing detection system using deep learning techniques . https://doi.org/10.1007/s10586-022-03604-4 Muhammad Shafiq, Zhaoquan Gu, Omar Cheikhrouhou et al. (2022). The Rise of "Internet of Things": Review and Open Research Issues Related to Detection and Prevention of IoT-Based Security Attacks . https://doi.org/10.1155/2022/8669348 Abbas M. Al-Ghaili, Hairoladenan Kasim, Naif Mohammed Al-Hada et al. (2022). A Review of Metaverse's Definitions, Architecture, Applications, Challenges, Issues, Solutions, and Future Trends . https://doi.org/10.1109/access.2022.3225638 Hossein Abroshan, Jan Devos, Geert Poels et al. (2021). Phishing Happens Beyond Technology: The Effects of Human Behaviors and Demographics on Each Step of a Phishing Process . https://doi.org/10.1109/access.2021.3066383 Jason Thomas (2018). Individual Cyber Security: Empowering Employees to Resist Spear Phishing to Prevent Identity Theft and Ransomware Attacks . https://doi.org/10.5539/ijbm.v13n6p1 Jean-Paul A. Yaacoub, Mohamad Noura, Hassan Noura et al. (2019). Securing internet of medical things systems: Limitations, issues and recommendations .

https://doi.org/10.1016/j.future.2019.12.028 Gautami Tripathi, Mohd Abdul Ahad, Gabriella Casalino (2023). A comprehensive review of blockchain technology: Underlying principles and historical background with future challenges . https://doi.org/10.1016/j.dajour.2023.100344 Renee Shelby, Shalaleh Rismani, Kathryn Henne et al. (2023). Sociotechnical Harms of Algorithmic Systems: Scoping a Taxonomy for Harm Reduction . https://doi.org/10.1145/3600211.3604673 P. S. Aithal (2023). How to Create Business Value Through Technological Innovations Using ICCT Underlying Technologies . https://doi.org/10.47992/ijaeml.2581.7000.0184 Sean Brooks, Michael Garcia, Naomi Lefkovitz et al. (2017). An introduction to privacy engineering and risk management in federal systems . https://doi.org/10.6028/nist.ir.8062 Jamin Rahman Jim, Md. Tanzib Hosain, M. F. Mridha et al. (2023). Toward Trustworthy Metaverse: Advancements and Challenges . https://doi.org/10.1109/access.2023.3326258 Michael S. Mireles (2025). A Quiet Revolution in Intellectual Property Value and Protection: Cybersecurity Law's Continuing Rise . https://doi.org/10.60095/kfen8241 Keränen, Tiina (2025). Adoption of AI in Finnish Small and Medium size Enterprises : AI opportunities, challenges and misconceptions . https://openalex.org/W7112326524 Abdul Basit, Maham Zafar, Xuan Liu et al. (2020). A comprehensive survey of AI-enabled phishing attacks detection techniques . https://doi.org/10.1007/s11235-020-00733-2 Rana Alabdan (2020). Phishing Attacks Survey: Types, Vectors, and Technical Approaches . https://doi.org/10.3390/fi12100168 Felipe Romero Moreno (2024). Generative AI and deepfakes: a human rights approach to tackling harmful content . https://doi.org/10.1080/13600869.2024.2324540 Vasiliki Demertzi, Stavros Demertzis, Konstantinos Demertzis (2023). An Overview of Cyber Threats, Attacks and Countermeasures on the Primary Domains of Smart Cities . https://doi.org/10.3390/app13020790 Chanapha Butpheng, Kuo-

Hui Yeh, Hu Xiong (2020). Security and Privacy in IoT-Cloud-Based e-Health Systems—A Comprehensive Review . https://doi.org/10.3390/sym12071191 Mehdi Hazrati, Rozita Dara, Jasmin Kaur (2022). On-Farm Data Security: Practical Recommendations for Securing Farm Data . https://doi.org/10.3389/fsufs.2022.884187 Youssef Yamout, Tashaffi Samin Yeasar, Shahrear Iqbal et al. (2023). Beyond Smart Homes: An In-Depth Analysis of Smart Aging Care System Security . https://doi.org/10.1145/3610225 Tyler W. Moore, Christian W. Probst, Kai Rannenberg et al. (2017). Assessing ICT Security Risks in Socio-Technical Systems (Dagstuhl Seminar 16461) . https://doi.org/10.4230/dagrep.6.11.63 Wanling Cai, Liliana Pasquale, Kushal Ramkumar et al. (2025). Human-centric security for smart homes: A scoping review . https://doi.org/10.1016/j.cose.2025.104762 Nicole Girvan (2020). An Investigation into the Privacy and Security Risks of Smart Toys in New Zealand . https://openalex.org/W3033946961 Olivia Faria (2020). Internet of Torment: The Governance of Smart Home Technologies Against Technology-Facilitated Violence . https://doi.org/10.22215/etd/2020-14189 Emre Yıldırım, Remzi Altunışık, Doğa Ekrem Doğancı et al. (2025). Digital Ethics in Marketing . https://openalex.org/W7137715140 Unknown author (2025). Digital Ethics in Marketing . https://doi.org/10.59537/saupress.2447 Isabel García-Álvarez, Adrian Didiu (2025). ETHICOMP 2025 22nd international conference on the ethical and social impacts of ICT Lisbon . https://doi.org/10.26619/978-989-9002-62-3 Sobhy M. Abdelkader, Jeremiah Amissah, Sammy Kinga et al. (2024). Securing modern power systems: Implementing comprehensive strategies to enhance resilience and reliability against cyber-attacks . https://doi.org/10.1016/j.rineng.2024.102647 Tymoteusz Miller, Irmina Durlik, Ewelina Kostecka et al. (2025). Integrating Artificial Intelligence Agents with the Internet of Things for Enhanced Environmental Monitoring: Applications in Water Quality and Climate Data . https://

doi.org/10.3390/electronics14040696 Yang Yang, Kun Hua (2019). Emerging Technologies for 5G-Enabled Vehicular Networks . https://doi.org/10.1109/access.2019.2954466 Mohammad Tahir, Mohamed Hadi Habaebi, Mohammad Dabbagh et al. (2020). A Review on Application of Blockchain in 5G and Beyond Networks: Taxonomy, Field-Trials, Challenges and Opportunities . https://doi.org/10.1109/access.2020.3003020 Syed Agha Hassnain Mohsan, Qurat ul ain Zahra, Muhammad Asghar Khan et al. (2022). Role of Drone Technology Helping in Alleviating the COVID-19 Pandemic . https://doi.org/10.3390/mi13101593 Ahmed Aghmadi, Hossam M. Hussein, Ketulkumar Hitesh Polara et al. (2023). A Comprehensive Review of Architecture, Communication, and Cybersecurity in Networked Microgrid Systems . https://doi.org/10.3390/inventions8040084 Carl J. Dahlman, Sam Mealy, Martin Wermelinger (2016). Harnessing the digital economy for developing countries . https://doi.org/10.1787/4adffb24-en Adhirath Kapoor, Ankur Gupta, Rajesh Gupta et al. (2021). Ransomware Detection, Avoidance, and Mitigation Scheme: A Review and Future Directions . https://doi.org/10.3390/su14010008 Badis Hammi, Sherali Zeadally, Jamel Nebhen (2023). Security Threats, Countermeasures, and Challenges of Digital Supply Chains . https://doi.org/10.1145/3588999 Mohamed Rahouti, Kaiqi Xiong, Yufeng Xin et al. (2022). SDN Security Review: Threat Taxonomy, Implications, and Open Challenges . https://doi.org/10.1109/access.2022.3168972 Nawari Nawari, Shriraam Ravindran (2019). Blockchain and Building Information Modeling (BIM): Review and Applications in Post-Disaster Recovery . https://doi.org/10.3390/buildings9060149 Lewis Golightly, Paolo Modesti, Rémi Garcia et al. (2023). Securing distributed systems: A survey on access control techniques for cloud, blockchain, IoT and SDN . https://doi.org/10.1016/j.csa.2023.100015 Javeriah Saleem, Rafiqul Islam, Muhammad Ashad Kabir (2022). The Anonymity of the

Dark Web: A Survey . https://doi.org/10.1109/access.2022.3161547 Balaji Adusupalli, Sneha Singireddy, Harish Kumar Sriram et al. (2021). Revolutionizing Risk Assessment and Financial Ecosystems with Smart Automation, Secure Digital Solutions, and Advanced Analytical Frameworks . https://doi.org/10.31586/ujfe.2021.1297 Rahime Belen-Saglam, Enes Altuncu, Yang Lü et al. (2023). A systematic literature review of the tension between the GDPR and public blockchain systems . https://doi.org/10.1016/j.bcra.2023.100129 Nisha Rawindaran, Ambikesh Jayal, Edmond Prakash et al. (2021). Cost Benefits of Using Machine Learning Features in NIDS for Cyber Security in UK Small Medium Enterprises (SME) . https://doi.org/10.3390/fi13080186 Jothi Prakash, S. Arul Antran Vijay, Jegathesh Peatchimuthu (2023). The realm of metaverse: A survey . https://doi.org/10.1002/cav.2150 G. E. Vardakis, George Hatzivasilis, Eleftheria Koutsaki et al. (2024). Review of Smart-Home Security Using the Internet of Things . https://doi.org/10.3390/electronics13163343 Ahmed Arafa, Haytham A. Sheerah, Shada Alsalamah (2023). Emerging Digital Technologies in Healthcare with a Spotlight on Cybersecurity: A Narrative Review . https://doi.org/10.3390/info14120640 Paul Reedy (2023). Interpol review of digital evidence for 2019–2022 . https://doi.org/10.1016/j.fsisyn.2022.100313 James Pierce, Sarah Fox, Nick Merrill et al. (2018). Differential Vulnerabilities and a Diversity of Tactics . https://doi.org/10.1145/3274408 Saman Iftikhar (2024). Cyberterrorism as a global threat: a review on repercussions and countermeasures . https://doi.org/10.7717/peerj-cs.1772 Lavinia Mihaela Cristea (2020). Current security threats in the national and international context . https://doi.org/10.24818/jamis.2020.02007 Verena Zimmermann, Karen Renaud (2019). Moving from a 'human-as-problem" to a 'human-as-solution" cybersecurity mindset . https://doi.org/10.1016/j.ijhcs.2019.05.005 Marianne Junger, Lorena Montoya, F.-J. Overink (2016). Priming and warnings are not effective to prevent social engineering attacks . https://doi.org/10.1016/j.chb.2016.09.012 Abdul Rehman Javed, Yousaf Bin Zikria, Saif Ur Rehman et al. (2021). Future Smart Cities: Requirements, Emerging Technologies, Applications, Challenges, and Future Aspects . https://doi.org/10.36227/techrxiv.14722854.v1 Lázaro Florido-Benítez (2024). The types of hackers and cyberattacks in the aviation industry . https://doi.org/10.1007/s12198-024-00281-9 Manikant Thakur (2024). Cyber Security Threats and Countermeasures in Digital Age . https://doi.org/10.54060/a2zjournals.jase.42 Petar Radanliev (2024). Cyber diplomacy: defining the opportunities for cybersecurity and risks from Artificial Intelligence, IoT, Blockchains, and Quantum Computing . https://doi.org/10.1080/23742917.2024.2312671 Marco Eichelberg, Klaus Kleber, Marc Kämmerer (2020). Cybersecurity in PACS and Medical Imaging: an Overview . https://doi.org/10.1007/s10278-020-00393-3 Gareth Mott, Sarah Turner, Jason R. C. Nurse et al. (2023). Between a rock and a hard(ening) place: Cyber insurance in the ransomware era . https://doi.org/10.1016/j.cose.2023.103162 Barteková, Eva, Börkey, Peter (2022). Digitalisation for the transition to a resource efficient and circular economy . https://doi.org/10.1787/6f6d18e7-en Peter Mayer, Yixin Zou, Byron Lowens et al. (2023). Awareness, Intention, (In)Action: Individuals' Reactions to Data Breaches . https://doi.org/10.1145/3589958 Qiang Wang, Min Su, Min Zhang et al. (2021). Integrating Digital Technologies and Public Health to Fight Covid-19 Pandemic: Key Technologies, Applications, Challenges and Outlook of Digital Healthcare . https://doi.org/10.3390/ijerph18116053 Amr Adel (2023). Unlocking the Future: Fostering Human–Machine Collaboration and Driving Intelligent Automation through Industry 5.0 in Smart Cities . https://doi.org/10.3390/smartcities6050124 Bo Bian, Michaela Pagel, Huan Tang et al. (2023). Consumer Surveillance and Financial Fraud . https://doi.org/10.3386/w31692 P. S. Aithal, Vinay V. Prabhu (2025). The

Evolution of Banking Industry in India: Past, Present, and Future with Special Emphasis on the Impact of AI on Banking Operations . https://doi.org/10.64818/pijtrcs.3107.8494.0018 Nicole Nguyen (2019). “The Eyes and Ears on Our Frontlines”: Policing without Police to Counter Violent Extremism . https://doi.org/10.24908/ss.v17i3/4.8142 Banerjee, Indradip, Gupta, Shibakali, Bhattacharyya, Siddhartha (2019). Big Data Security . https://doi.org/10.1515/9783110606058 Wade Baker (2017). Toward a Decision Support System for Measuring and Managing Cybersecurity Risk in Supply Chains . https://openalex.org/W2905214471 Unknown author (2024). EXAMINING THE SECURITY ESSENCES OF INTERNET OF THINGS (IOT) DEVICES IN SMART HOMES: CHALLENGES, VULNERABILITIES, AND COUNTERMEASURES . https://doi.org/10.48009/1_iis_2024_123 Funmilola Olubunmi Omotayo (2025). Information Security Awareness and Behavior of Smartphone Users in the Ibadan Metropolis, Nigeria . https://doi.org/10.62915/2472-2707.1240 Adeleye Dupe Ayesha, Prof. Abd. Rahman Ahlan, Najhan Muhammad Ibrahim (2026). E-Government Adoption in West Africa: A Narrative Review of Trends, Challenges, and Policy Innovations . https://doi.org/10.51584/ijrias.2026.110200065 Pravik Solanki, John Grundy, Waqar Hussain (2022). Operationalising ethics in artificial intelligence for healthcare: a framework for AI developers . https://doi.org/10.1007/s43681-022-00195-z Reeshad S. Dalal, David Howard, Rebecca J. Bennett et al. (2021). Organizational science and cybersecurity: abundant opportunities for research at the interface . https://doi.org/10.1007/s10869-021-09732-9 Michael Mylrea, Nikki Robinson (2023). Artificial Intelligence (AI) Trust Framework and Maturity Model: Applying an Entropy Lens to Improve Security, Privacy, and Ethical AI . https://doi.org/10.3390/e25101429 Yves Barlette, Annabelle Jaouen, Paméla Baillette (2020). Bring Your Own Device (BYOD) as reversed IT adoption: Insights into managers' coping strategies . https://doi.org/10.1016/j.ijinfomgt.2020.102212 Susanne Barth, Dan Ionita, Pieter Hartel (2022). Understanding Online Privacy—A Systematic Review of Privacy Visualizations and Privacy by Design Guidelines . https://doi.org/10.1145/3502288 Bilal Naqvi, Kseniia Perova, Ali Farooq et al. (2023). Mitigation strategies against the phishing attacks: A systematic literature review . https://doi.org/10.1016/j.cose.2023.103387 Salem Argaw, Nefti-Eboni Bempong, Bruce Eshaya-Chauvin et al. (2019). The state of research on cyberattacks against hospitals and available best practice recommendations: a scoping review . https://doi.org/10.1186/s12911-018-0724-5 Tracy Tam, Asha Rao, Joanne L. Hall (2021). The good, the bad and the missing: A Narrative review of cyber-security implications for australian small businesses . https://doi.org/10.1016/j.cose.2021.102385 Toby Walsh (2019). The effective and ethical development of artificial intelligence: an opportunity to improve our wellbeing . https://openalex.org/W2965948505 Shereen Ismail, Diana W. Dawoud, Hassan Reza (2023). Securing Wireless Sensor Networks Using Machine Learning and Blockchain: A Review . https://doi.org/10.3390/fi15060200 Theo Lynn, John G. Mooney, Pierangelo Rosati et al. (2018). Disrupting Finance . https://doi.org/10.1007/978-3-030-02330-0 Naeem Allah Rakha (2024). Cybercrime and the Law: Addressing the Challenges of Digital Forensics in Criminal Investigations . https://doi.org/10.22201/iij.24485306e.2024.2.18892 Ijaz Ahmad, Felipe Rodríguez, Tanesh Kumar et al. (2024). Communications Security in Industry X: A Survey . https://doi.org/10.1109/ojcoms.2024.3356076 Eklas Hossain, Imtiaj Khan, Fuad Un-Noor et al. (2019). Application of Big Data and Machine Learning in Smart Grid, and Associated Security Concerns: A Review . https://doi.org/10.1109/access.2019.2894819 Angelos I. Stoumpos, Fotis Kitsios, Michael A. Talias (2023). Digital Transformation in Healthcare: Technology Acceptance and Its

Applications . https://doi.org/10.3390/ijerph20043407 Julia Prümmer, Tommy van Steen, Bibi van den Berg (2023). A systematic review of current cybersecurity training methods . https://doi.org/10.1016/j.cose.2023.103585 Bonnie Buchanan, Danika Wright (2021). The impact of machine learning on UK financial services . https://doi.org/10.1093/oxrep/grab016 Ricardo M. Czekster, Paul Grace, César Marcon et al. (2023). Challenges and Opportunities for Conducting Dynamic Risk Assessments in Medical IoT . https://doi.org/10.3390/app13137406 Samson O. Oruma, Yonas Zewdu Ayele, Fabien Sechi et al. (2023). Security Aspects of Social Robots in Public Spaces: A Systematic Mapping Study . https://doi.org/10.3390/s23198056 Joint Task Force Transformation Initiative (2020). Security and Privacy Controls for Information Systems and Organizations . https://doi.org/10.6028/nist.sp.800-53r5-draft Bilgin Metin, Fatma Gül Özhan, Martín Wynn (2024). Digitalisation and Cybersecurity: Towards an Operational Framework . https://doi.org/10.3390/electronics13214226 Scott Shackelford, Scott Russell, Jeffrey Haut (2015). Bottoms Up: A Comparison of Voluntary Cybersecurity Frameworks . https://openalex.org/W2295344968 Nadhira Khezami, Nourcherif Gharbi, Bilel Neji et al. (2022). Blockchain Technology Implementation in the Energy Sector: Comprehensive Literature Review and Mapping . https://doi.org/10.3390/su142315826 Saqib Saeed, Sarah A. Suayyid, Manal S. Al-Ghamdi et al. (2023). A Systematic Literature Review on Cyber Threat Intelligence for Organizational Cybersecurity Resilience . https://doi.org/10.3390/s23167273 Nadir Naveed Ahmed, Krishnadas Nanath (2021). Exploring Cybersecurity Ecosystem in the Middle East: Towards an SME Recommender System . https://doi.org/10.13052/jcsm2245-1439.1032 Daniel Bendler, Michael Felderer (2022). Competency Models for Information Security and Cybersecurity Professionals: Analysis of Existing Work and a New Model . https://doi.org/10.1145/3573205

Αναστάσιος Παπαθανασίου, George Liontos, Athanasios Katsouras et al. (2024). Cybersecurity Guide for SMEs: Protecting Small and Medium-Sized Enterprises in the Digital Era . https://doi.org/10.4236/jis.2025.161001 Dennis C. Acuña (2016). Enterprise Computer Security: A Literature Review . https://doi.org/10.17705/3jmwa.00016 Patrick O'Reilly, Kristina Rigopoulos, Larry Feldman et al. (2017). 2016 NIST/ITL cybersecurity program: annual report . https://doi.org/10.6028/nist.sp.800-195 Doreen Lynn Maahs (2018). Managerial Strategies Small Businesses Use to Prevent Cybercrime . https://openalex.org/W2909568322 International Panel on the Information Environment (IPIE), Benjamin Faveri, Maureen Johnson-León et al. (2025). Towards A Global AI Auditing Framework: Assessment and Recommendations . https://doi.org/10.61452/zwed1485 Hao-Ping Lee, Yu-Ju Yang, Thomas Şerban von Davier et al. (2023). Deepfakes, Phrenology, Surveillance, and More! A Taxonomy of AI Privacy Risks . https://doi.org/10.48550/arxiv.2310.07879 Samrat Acharya, Yury Dvorkin, Hrvoje Pandžić et al. (2020). Cybersecurity of Smart Electric Vehicle Charging: A Power Grid Perspective . https://doi.org/10.1109/access.2020.3041074

Conclusion

The habits in this book are meant to do more than prevent a single bad day. They are meant to change the conditions around your account so that mistakes are less likely, damage is easier to contain, and recovery is less chaotic when something still goes wrong. That shift matters because social media harm rarely stays neatly inside one app. It can move through your contacts, your content, your connected tools, and the trust other people place in your name. A breach, impersonation, or privacy lapse often creates cascading effects, which is why the best protection is built as a system rather than as a one-time fix [17].

By now, the central pattern should be clear: the most useful security decisions are usually the ones made before pressure arrives. A strong password helps only if it is unique and supported by a safer recovery path. Privacy settings help only if they are reviewed with the same care you give to public posts. Scam detection helps only if you slow down enough to verify before acting. Device hygiene helps only if the device itself is treated as part of the account. None of these measures works perfectly on its own, but together they reduce the number of easy openings an attacker can use.

That is also why social media safety has to remain practical. If your process is too complicated, you will not keep using it. If it is too rigid, you will eventually bypass it. The right standard is not maximum restriction; it is reliable control. You want to know who can reach you, what can be seen, which tools can act on your behalf, and how to respond when those conditions change. In other words, you are not trying to eliminate risk entirely. You are trying to make risk visible, manageable, and harder to exploit.

Artificial intelligence will only make that discipline more important. The same systems that can help people write, organize, analyze, and automate can also help attackers scale deception, imitate voices, and generate more convincing lures [5][12]. Deepfake-style manipulation increases the value of verification habits because seeing or hearing something familiar is no longer enough on its own [4]. When content can be fabricated quickly and distributed widely, trust has to rest on more than appearance. It has to rest on process: checking sources, confirming requests, and resisting the pressure to react instantly.

For individuals, that means protecting personal identity and daily routine. For creators, it means guarding the credibility that keeps an audience engaged. For small businesses, it means preserving customer trust, message integrity, and operational access. Those are different uses of social media, but they all depend on the same core idea: your account is part communication channel, part reputation surface, and part access point. If any one of those parts is neglected, the others become easier to exploit.

The goal from here is not to become suspicious of everything. It is to become deliberate. Check the setting before the post. Confirm the sender before the click. Review the session before the damage spreads. Keep the recovery path current. Remove what you no longer need. Teach the people around you to do the same. When those behaviors become ordinary, security stops feeling like an emergency response and starts functioning like a stable part of how you use the platform.

That is the standard this book has tried to build: not fear, but readiness; not isolation, but control; not perfection, but resilience. If you keep those priorities in place, your social media presence becomes much harder to misuse and much easier to defend when conditions change.

Appendix: Quick-Reference Tools and Checklists

This appendix is designed for the moments when you do not want to search through a chapter to find the next right move. The tools and checklists that follow condense the book's main protective habits into formats you can use during routine maintenance, a privacy review, or a fast response to something suspicious. They are meant to support decision-making under pressure, when attention is limited and clarity matters most. Security guidance is more effective when it is easy to repeat and easy to verify, and structured checklists are one of the simplest ways to turn that principle into action [151][283][287]. Use these pages as a working aid, not a one-time read-through: mark them up, adapt them to your own accounts, and keep them close enough to consult before small mistakes become larger problems.

Account security checklist

Start with the credentials themselves. Every important social account should have a unique password that is long, random, and stored in a password manager rather than remembered by habit or recycled from another service. Reuse is one of the most common ways a single mistake becomes a larger compromise, because one exposed password can unlock more than one platform. If you are still relying on variations of the same phrase, the checklist should treat that as unfinished work, not a minor weakness. Change the password after any sign of exposure, after sharing access with someone who no longer needs it, and after a device loss or malware incident. For shared business accounts, make sure the password is not known to former employees, contractors, or anyone who no longer has an active role.

Next, turn on multi-factor authentication everywhere it is offered, and prefer the strongest method the platform supports. An authenticator app or hardware security key is generally more resistant to interception than a text message, which can be vulnerable to phone-number takeover or message forwarding. The point is not to collect security features for their own sake; it is to make unauthorized access harder even when a password is guessed, stolen, or phished. If a platform gives you a choice, do not leave the safest option unused because it takes an extra minute to set up. That minute is part of the cost of reducing risk. Keep backup codes in a secure place, separate from the device you use every day, so a lost phone does not become a locked account.

Recovery settings deserve the same level of attention as sign-in settings, because recovery is often the path attackers target once they realize the password alone is no longer enough. Review the email address and phone number attached to account recovery and confirm that both are current, controlled by you, and protected with their own strong authentication. Remove any old email account that you no longer monitor and any phone number that has been replaced. If the platform offers trusted contacts or recovery approvals, choose people who are reliable, reachable, and unlikely to be pressured by a scammer pretending to be you. Recovery planning should also include a quick test: can you still access the recovery mailbox, can you still receive the code, and do you know where the backup codes are stored? If not, the account is only partially protected.

Review active sessions and logged-in devices on a regular schedule, not only after something looks suspicious. Most platforms show where the account is currently signed in, which devices are connected, and sometimes the approximate location or browser type. Look for sessions you do not recognize, devices you no longer use, and old browsers that should have been signed out months ago. If you find something unexpected, end the session immediately and change the password before assuming the problem is over. This is especially important after travel, device replacement, or use of a shared computer. A forgotten session can remain open long after you have stopped thinking about it, and an open session can bypass the normal sign-in barrier entirely.

Connected apps and third-party tools should be treated as part of the account, not as harmless extras. Scheduling tools, analytics dashboards, browser extensions, social media management platforms, and shopping integrations often request broad permissions because they need to post, read, or interact on your behalf. That convenience creates a security tradeoff: if the tool is compromised, misconfigured, or no longer needed, it can become a back door into your presence. Review every connected app and remove anything you do not actively use, do not recognize, or do not trust enough to keep linked. Pay close attention to tools that can send messages, publish posts, access direct messages, or manage advertising and payment functions. In a business setting, make sure each tool has a named owner and a clear reason for existing. Research on cybersecurity resilience consistently shows that reducing unnecessary access and improving visibility into risk helps organizations respond more effectively [291].

Login alerts are useful only if you act on them quickly and do not train yourself to ignore them. If the platform notifies you of a new sign-in, treat it as a prompt to verify, not as background noise. Confirm whether the device, browser, time, and location match your own activity.

If they do not, assume the account may already be exposed and move into containment: sign out of other sessions, change the password, review recovery settings, and check for unauthorized changes to the profile, messages, or connected apps. Do the same after a password reset request you did not initiate. Fast response matters because account abuse often spreads through trust, not just through access.

Finally, make the checklist practical enough that you will actually use it. A perfect security plan that lives in a note you never open is less useful than a shorter routine you complete every month. For a personal account, that may mean passwords, MFA, recovery settings, active sessions, and connected apps. For a creator or business account, add role review, shared access, delegated tools, and backup contact verification. If the process feels too large, split it into small passes and schedule them. Security is strongest when account protection becomes a repeatable habit instead of a one-time cleanup.

Privacy audit worksheet

A privacy audit works best when it is treated as a deliberate review of exposure, not as a quick scan through settings. The goal is to see your account the way an outsider would: what can be learned from the profile itself, what can be inferred from your activity, and what can be reached through connected features that you may have forgotten were turned on. For individuals, creators, and small businesses alike, this kind of review matters because cyber risk is rarely limited to one obvious weakness. It is usually the combination of a few ordinary choices that creates the problem [292] [294].

Begin with the basic visibility of the account. Ask who can see your profile, your posts, your stories, your comments, and your follower or friend list. Then check whether the platform is making it easier than you intended for strangers to find you through search, phone contacts, email lookup, or recommendations. If your account is public by necessity, narrow the scope elsewhere: limit what appears in the bio, remove details that are not needed for recognition, and make sure profile photos, headers, and pinned content do not expose routines, locations, or internal business information. A profile does not need to be bare to be safer; it needs to be intentional.

Next, review the information that other people can add to your profile or attach to your name. Tagging, mentions, photo approvals, story resharing, and comment visibility can all expand your exposure without you publishing anything new yourself. If you manage a brand or creator account, this step is especially important because a single tagged image, customer comment, or public reply can reveal more than the original post. Tightening these controls reduces the chance that someone else can use your account as a distribution point for unwanted detail, confusion, or impersonation.

Location-related settings deserve a separate pass. Check whether the app can access your device location, whether posts are being geotagged automatically, and whether discovery features are making it easier for people to connect your online identity with a physical place. Even when a platform does not publish exact coordinates, repeated clues can still be enough to reveal where you live, work, travel, or spend time. That matters because location data is often most useful to attackers when it is combined with timing, routines, and public interactions rather than viewed as a single isolated clue.

Then move to data sharing beyond the visible profile. Review contact syncing, ad personalization, off-platform activity tracking, third-party logins, and any connected apps that can read, post, or manage content on your behalf. These settings are easy to leave in place because they feel like convenience features, but they often widen the amount of information the platform or a partner service can collect and use. If a connected app no longer serves a clear purpose, remove it. If the platform offers a way to limit ad targeting or reduce data use for recommendations, turn those options down to the lowest level that still supports the way you use the service.

Account recovery is part of privacy because it determines who can take control when access is challenged. Verify the email address and phone number tied to recovery, remove anything that is outdated, and make sure the recovery path does not route through a shared inbox or a number you no longer monitor. Check whether backup codes exist and where they are stored. Review trusted devices and active sessions as well, since a forgotten login on an old phone or browser can become a quiet access point long after you stop using it. Small businesses should treat this step as a continuity issue, not a convenience issue, because weak recovery settings can turn a temporary problem into a full loss of control [294] [110].

As you work through the audit, write down only the settings that need action, not every detail you inspect. A useful worksheet captures the platform, the setting, the current status, the risk it creates, and the change you plan to make. For example: "Instagram, story replies, open to everyone, unnecessary contact from strangers, restrict to followers." This keeps the review practical and repeatable. It also helps you notice patterns across platforms, such as using the same recovery email everywhere, leaving contact syncing enabled by habit, or allowing public discovery on accounts that do not need it. Over time, the audit becomes less about chasing every new feature and more about maintaining a stable boundary around what your account reveals.

Use this worksheet format:

Platform: Which account are you reviewing?

Setting or feature: What control are you checking?

Current status: What is it set to now?

Risk or exposure: What could someone learn, do, or infer?
Action needed: Change, remove, limit, or verify.
Review date: When will you check it again?

Incident response quick guide

The first minutes after a suspected breach are for containment, not for perfect diagnosis. If you are still trying to decide whether the problem is "real," assume it is serious enough to justify immediate action. The safest response is to move from observation to control: stop new damage, preserve access if you still have it, and reduce the number of places the attacker can continue operating. That may mean changing the password from a trusted device, revoking active sessions, turning off any linked automation, and securing the recovery email before you do anything else. If the account is already posting, messaging, or following people without your permission, treat every minute as part of the incident window.

Your first task is to cut off the most obvious paths of continued access. If you can still sign in, change the password immediately and enable or re-check multi-factor authentication if it is not already active. Do not reuse an old password or a similar variation, because attackers often test predictable substitutions first. Next, review the account's active sessions and log out of everything you do not recognize. If the platform allows it, force sign-out from all devices. Then inspect recovery settings, phone numbers, and email addresses for changes you did not make. A compromised recovery path can be more dangerous than the password itself because it gives the attacker a way back in after you think the problem is solved.

If the account is connected to other tools, disconnect them in a deliberate order. Scheduling apps, analytics tools, browser extensions, and cross-posting services may still have valid access even after you change the main password. Attackers often use those connections to keep posting or to regain control indirectly. Remove anything you do not need right now, especially if you do not fully recognize the permission level it has. If the breach involved a business or creator account, check whether ad tools, payment methods, shop integrations, or team roles were altered. A social account can be the entry point, but the damage often spreads into other services that share trust with it.

Once the account is contained, preserve evidence before you clean up too much. Save screenshots of suspicious posts, messages, profile changes, login alerts, and any email notifications related to password resets or recovery changes. Capture usernames, timestamps, URLs, and visible identifiers. If the attacker deleted content or changed the profile image, document what you can still see through cached views, notifications, or messages from other users. This matters because incident response depends on sequence: what happened first, what changed next, and where the unauthorized activity appeared. Clear documentation also makes it easier to report the abuse to the platform and, when necessary, to partners, customers, or law enforcement.

Then report the incident through the platform's official channels using the clearest version of events you can provide. Stick to facts: the account name, the time you noticed the compromise, what unauthorized actions occurred, and what steps you already took. Avoid emotional language or speculation. If the attacker used the account to send phishing messages, scam followers, or impersonate your brand, say so plainly. If you are a small business or creator, notify any connected collaborators whose accounts or tools may also be at risk. Cyber harm often propagates through trust relationships, and information sharing between affected parties is one of the few ways to limit that spread [17][137].

Communication with your audience should be brief, accurate, and updated only as facts become clear. If followers, customers, or partners may have received malicious messages, warn them not to click links or share codes that came from the compromised account. If the account is temporarily unavailable, say that you are addressing a security issue and will post updates from a verified channel. Do not overexplain the technical details or speculate about how the breach happened until you have checked the evidence. A calm, direct notice protects people better than silence, but a rushed or contradictory statement can create confusion that the attacker benefits from.

After the immediate threat is under control, review what allowed the breach to succeed and what needs to change before you return to normal use. That review should include the login method, recovery options, connected apps, device security, and any recent messages or links that may have triggered the compromise. If the incident exposed personal data, location clues, or business access, treat those as separate risks that may require additional monitoring. The goal is not just to restore the account; it is to make the next incident harder to launch and easier to contain.

Recommended review schedule

A review schedule only works if it matches the pace at which social media risk actually changes. Some threats are constant, but the details shift quickly: new device logins appear, connected apps gain or lose permissions, platform settings change, and old recovery methods stop being reliable. That is why the right schedule is not simply "check everything often." It is a layered routine that gives urgent items frequent attention while reserving deeper reviews for less frequent, more deliberate inspections. The point is to catch drift before it becomes exposure.

For most users, a weekly review should be short and focused. Look for anything that suggests active change rather than long-term maintenance: unfamiliar login alerts, new direct messages that request action, unexpected follower growth from suspicious accounts, posts you do not remember publishing, or account notices that mention policy, payment, or security. This is also the right time to glance at active sessions if the platform makes them easy to see. The weekly check should not become a full audit. It should answer one question: does anything look different enough to require immediate attention?

A monthly review should go deeper. This is the point at which you verify the controls that tend to drift quietly in the background. Confirm that your password is still unique and stored in your password manager. Check that multi-factor authentication is still enabled and that the recovery email and phone number still belong to you. Review trusted devices, active sessions, and connected apps, then remove anything you no longer use. If you manage a business or creator account, this is also the time to confirm that anyone with access still needs it. Shared access often becomes stale without anyone noticing, and stale access is a common source of avoidable risk. Controlled and restrictive access is a basic resilience measure, not an optional preference [137].

Quarterly reviews should be broader and more deliberate. Step back and ask whether your account structure still matches the way you actually use the platform. Maybe you started with one account and now use it for personal, professional, and promotional activity. Maybe you linked tools months ago for convenience and never revisited them. Maybe your audience, posting habits, or business workflow changed, but your privacy boundaries did not. A quarterly review is the right moment to reassess those assumptions. It is also a good time to compare your profile, recovery paths, and connected services against the list of things you most need to protect, so that your security effort stays aligned with your real priorities rather than with old habits.

There are also event-driven reviews, and they matter just as much as calendar-based ones. If you travel, change phones, hire staff, launch a campaign, add a scheduling tool, receive a phishing attempt, or notice an unusual login, do not wait for the next monthly or quarterly checkpoint. Treat the event as a trigger for immediate verification. Social platforms are dynamic environments, and the surrounding ecosystem of devices, services, and third-party tools can change the exposure surface faster than a fixed schedule alone can catch [1][15]. A good review schedule is therefore not rigid. It is responsive.

For individuals, the schedule can stay simple: weekly for activity checks, monthly for access and recovery, quarterly for the full account and device review. For influencers and small teams, add a shared cadence for business-critical accounts, brand assets, and delegated access. If more than one person can post, approve, or respond, the review schedule should include a regular check of who has authority to do what. That prevents confusion later, especially during a high-pressure moment when old permissions are easy to forget and hard to unwind. In practice, this means keeping a small, current list of account owners, trusted devices, recovery methods, and connected tools, then checking that list on schedule rather than assuming it remains accurate.

The most useful review schedule is one you can repeat without making it a project. If the process feels heavy, people postpone it; if it feels vague, they skip the important parts. Keep the weekly review short enough to do in a few minutes, the monthly review structured enough to cover the essentials, and the quarterly review broad enough to catch changes in how you use the account. Over time, that rhythm reduces the chance that a forgotten setting, stale permission, or missed alert turns into a larger problem.

www.ingramcontent.com/pod-product-compliance
Lightning Source LLC
LaVergne TN
LVHW100316210926
848480LV00003B/1143
* 9 7 8 1 7 6 4 7 1 1 1 2 8 *